ALSO BY CAROL BARBOUR

What The World Needs Now ... 90 Days to a Happier Life

I Chose Defiance

Carol Barbour

2018 by Carol Barbour
All rights reserved.
No part of this book may be reproduced, in any form,
without written permission from the publisher.

Published in the United States by Amazon, 2018

Library of Congress Cataloging-In-Publication Data

Barbour, Carol, 1969-
I Chose Defiance/Carol Barbour

For my mother, my first teacher, my inspiration to become an educator and my heart;

In loving memory of my godmother, Soror Martha Askew, a stellar woman;

For the loved ones who've stood by and believed in me through it all.

FOREWORD

"When your intentions are good and you start to drive, where does your navigational system take you?"

Donna M. N. Edwards, J. D.

From about 1916 to 1970 more than six million African Americans moved from the rural South to the cities of the North, Midwest and West and this phenomenon was called "The Great Migration". They moved because it was their belief that they would have a better life. In mid-2007, in District of Columbia Public Schools (DCPS), our political leaders sought to take a similar leap and created what I will call "The Great Education" movement. Supposedly, it was created to improve public educational services to District residents. Unfortunately, rather than develop well thought out, consistent, long term improvements that would truly benefit the children they served, a headline-grabbing "You're Fired" approach was adopted. Simply stated, they did what *looks* good as opposed to what *is* good.

To lead this effort as Chancellor of DCPS, they tapped an "outsider," a tough, enthusiastic, yet unqualified young woman, and gave her unrestricted authority and power. Was this an early signal of what we are currently experiencing politically in this country?

It is difficult to ignore these glaring similarities. For example, allegations of grade tampering were treated as "trumped up charges" because they were not seen as common throughout the system. It was not clear if the suspicious scores and grades were used in the overall test data upon which educators were allegedly evaluated. There was never an explanation of *if* or *how* the students who got the bogus scores were being helped. In addition, the criteria for success changed as did the population of students in the schools.

In short, those who were deemed failing educators were not judged by the same criteria as those who replaced them. Even more disturbing is the fact that some educators who met the new criteria were still non-renewed because they were not "a good fit".

Years later as we reflect upon what happened, how has DCPS been affected? It has low rates of administrator and teacher retention and student enrollment has decreased. There are still poorly educated adults. And, there are administrators and educators whose reputations have been unjustly ruined. School buildings and properties have been sold and a number of charter schools with questionable results have emerged. The initial Chancellor for Change has faded into virtual anonymity as the educational pundits and financial backers who once glorified her efforts have since re-evaluated the outcomes and withdrawn their support.

The setting of this book begins during the first year in the era of "The Great Education". There are literally hundreds of stories that *could* be told. This one is compelling because it includes police and school corruption, greed, sex, redemption, and defiance. It leaves us to consider the question first raised, "When your intentions are good and you start to drive, where does your navigational system take you?" The answer is clear – it leads to the destination preceded by the road paved with all good intentions. Yet a phoenix rises from the ashes of this fire to tell her story and invite a call to action.

TABLE OF CONTENTS

PART ONE: BROKEN

CHAPTER ONE		Keep One Eye Open
CHAPTER TWO		The List
CHAPTER THREE		What Lies Beneath
CHAPTER FOUR		Deeper Into the Rat Hole
CHAPTER FIVE		Pressure Points
CHAPTER SIX		Shark Bait

PART TWO: ROCK BOTTOM

CHAPTER SEVEN		The Dirty South
CHAPTER EIGHT		It Depends on Who You Ask
CHAPTER NINE		It's No Fun When the Rabbit Has the Gun
CHAPTER TEN		Fallout … Too Many Unanswered Questions

PART THREE: I'M NOT THE ONLY EDUCATOR ON A WIRE

CHAPTER ELEVEN		The Politics of Testing and Scandal
CHAPTER TWELVE		Now What?

PART FOUR: MADE WHOLE

CHAPTER THIRTEEN		Lessons Learned

INTRODUCTION

"The way I learned it, the kid in the schoolyard who doesn't
want to fight always leaves with a black eye.
If you indicate you'll do anything to avoid trouble,
that's when you get trouble."

Curtis James Jackson III

Imagine receiving a call from your immediate supervisor and being summoned to an unplanned meeting in May, one of the busiest months during the academic year. While navigating traffic, you contemplate possible reasons for the meeting. Instinctively, you realize impromptu sit-downs are rarely a positive omen. You arrive at the office anxiously, your stomach aflutter, dread punctuating every moment. Your supervisor's administrative assistant greets you with an uncharacteristically sympathetic expression. After waiting anxiously for what feels like a tense eternity the conference room door swings open and you're summoned in as one of your flustered colleagues departs. He or she doesn't make eye contact with you as they rush to the door without acknowledging you or anyone else.

Seated beside your supervisor at the conference table is a central office representative. As soon as you note this person's presence, your worst fears about a potential ambush are confirmed. After directing you to sit down, your supervisor begins the meeting abruptly in a cold, monotone voice. Adding insult to the injurious surprise, you're directed to read along silently while your supervisor reads a letter aloud, informing you the Chancellor no longer wants *you* to "serve" on her team. You hear the words as your supervisor reads the letter but you still can't quite wrap your mind around the message. Your heart races more rapidly than a stallion's at the starting gate during an opening race. Your stomach, turning and flipping, rivals the worst hangover. Your head pounds competitively, your skin burns with humiliation. You've *never* received any reprimands about your performance nor has there been any mention of an improvement plan. As your mind races, you think of your midyear evaluation. There wasn't any mention of performance concerns and you know you're supposed to receive notice if your performance is deficient as required by the collective bargaining agreement.

The final proverbial bomb drops. Your face burns as if singed by volcanic lava. Your supervisor demands that you, without time for consideration, decide whether you'll resign, retire or be fired. Each choice is a losing alternative because it's not your own. As you leave the meeting, your supervisor reminds you to continue doing your best through the end of the school year to serve the children, their parents and the faculty and staff. The students became the final mention at the end of an unanticipated constructive dismissal conference. It shouldn't be a surprise since children are usually the afterthought in central office politics. In a flash, a capricious decision made by an inexperienced, under-qualified, overpaid and habitually arrogant Chancellor changes your life, painting you as the boil on the butt of education across virtually every media outlet. It all took place with the thoughtless stroke of a pen and an unquenchable thirst for recognition and fame, all in the name of change.

Bewildered. Perplexed. Traumatized. Angry. Countless other emotions flood your mind as you haven't had a calm moment to process what just happened. As cliché as it sounds, you wonder when you'll awaken from this employment nightmare. You rush to your car because you need to be alone. Perhaps you punch the dashboard in a fit of rage or you grab the steering wheel, gripping it tightly. You might shake and surrender to the river of panic drowning you. Mustering the last reserve of your dignity to return to work, you're unsure what you'll encounter but you're resolved to survive the remainder of the day with your façade of control.

Other more predictable worries don't immediately haunt you but they'll seize the opportunity to terrorize you soon enough. Gradually, the experience becomes more a new reality than a surreal nightmare and you realize you have to begin applying for another position. The first logical step is to apply for a position in surrounding school systems. After completing online applications, your mind races and stalls as the days and weeks pass. You wait. Phone calls and emails finally come and you receive notification you've been selected to complete a screening interview. The invitation renews your dashed hopes. Once initial screening interviews are over, you return to the increasingly familiar sunken place of despair again because time has passed without follow-up calls or second interviews. When the letters and emails arrive, informing you that you're "not the right fit," you realize the odds had been stacked against you from the start. Not only had most school systems already completed their hiring process, you're also "one of those discarded principals," as several school systems in the region label you.

Time marches on. Perhaps you're facing foreclosure. You cringe when you receive utility bills and other expenses you can't meet. Your health insurance ends and since COBRA bears an exorbitant cost in light of all of the obligations you must now fulfill without a full, sustainable income, you no longer have health insurance. Health care costs are one of the leading causes of personal bankruptcy and the Affordable Health Care Act is still a dream deferred, entangled in bureaucratic arguments.

Now ... imagine each of these things happened to *you*.

The scenario I described isn't fictitious. It's an account of what happened to twenty-four unsuspecting principals in the District of Columbia Public Schools (DCPS) at the hand of former school system Chancellor Michelle Ann Rhee May 5, 2008, on an administrative whim. While serving in her official capacity, Michelle Rhee gleefully took full advantage of countless photo opportunities, paid speeches, interviews and personal appearances at the expense of the school system's students, their parents, communities and the school system's workforce while making ambitious career moves at the expense of those she and her subordinates chose to scapegoat. No one serving in an elected or appointed position in the Government of The District of Columbia at the time dared to question her or stand up to her beyond posturing at public meetings, writing letters and making ambitious sound bites over written and live media. Her defamatory words severely prejudiced public opinion and damaged countless professional reputations without consequence. Equally as troubling, there wasn't much deep thought or consideration from the many people who listened to her as captive audiences and believed her without a second thought. It was if there was a wrinkle in time where unreason became reason, the pre-Trump era of alternative facts.

  Just who is this Chancellor? She was a dilettante in educational leadership when former mayor Adrian M. Fenty removed the more educated, experienced and highly qualified Dr. Clifford B. Janey and replace him inexperience and unpredictability. In order to make the change fit the criteria for No Child Left Behind Legislation, Fenty replaced the position of superintendent with the more creative job title of chancellor as he assumed full control of the city's beleaguered schools, naming Rhee as its leader. A superintendent is an experienced educator who has served in progressive leadership positions and has earned the commensurate education and experience to hold the position according to state criteria. A chancellor is typically the chairperson of the school board and the manager of the school system and all of its departments. The educational and experience criteria governing a chancellor are much more loose and subjective.

Many people recognize Rhee's brand of reform as chancellor through the due diligence demonstrated by the Washington Post as they favorably chronicled her days in the District. The Post continuously published myriad articles virtually deifying her as the panacea American school children needed to thrive and survive. Rhee became a reality star with a fulltime side job. Evidence surfaced that proved just how strongly the Chancellor influenced the newspaper when a local reporter published a 2009 email detailing how Rhee commanded a positive editorial review for a favored staff member.

Rhee's words in multiple media outlets further underscored her actions. On July, 23 2008, the Chancellor bragged in an interview about her "tremendous will." She also shared that she focuses on the endgame and that if there are rules in the way, she will bend the rules. When I read *Ordinary Injustice: How America Holds Court*, a brilliant book by Amy Bach, I absorbed every word. The pervasive corruption in America continues to affect me greatly and it affects so many others too. I don't believe there is a culture of acceptance for corruption in our nation. Citizens who fight corruption become discouraged and worn down by motions to dismiss, stalling tactics and the antics they face while seeking justice. In 2008, this group of twenty-four DCPS principals lost their jobs in a mass firing while worked at the whims of this Chancellor. These twenty-four principals, thrown together in a mass firing, lost their jobs without timely evaluations and valid reasons. "You're fired" is all they heard, as if they were guest stars on the season finale of the reality show *The Apprentice*, ironic since Rhee became one of President Trump's top choices for Secretary of Education.

There is no doubt every organization should dismiss workers who perform poorly and no reasonable person questions that. However, when dismissing poorly performing workers, leaders should follow their organization's established rules, policies and procedures in doing so. Rhee did not. It doesn't take a full-blown defamation campaign and media blitz to terminate workers ethically and in accordance with established systemic procedures.

Each of these twenty-four principals has a unique, interesting back story to share. In this book, I'm sharing mine.

PART ONE: BROKEN

"The craziest things already happened to me, so either you'll be laughing at me or you're laughing with me, ha."

Nas
"No Introduction"

CHAPTER ONE:
Always Keep One Eye Open

How can you fairly assess something from the outside looking in?
There's gotta be them times you'll be wrong, nah mean?

Jay Z
Lucky Me

Public education policy and funding at the federal and state levels has been a longtime political crapshoot. Our political leaders place countless pitiable education wagers and the consequences of their careless bets often handicap our children. Historically, American politicians roll the dice willingly for new, sophisticated weaponry. They play blackjack for oil, spin the roulette wheel for land and airspace and pull slot machine leers for countless covert deals. We the people finance their long shots all too often without proper explanations in the name of our best interests, national security and freedom. They engage in these behaviors with masterful poker faces. Every priority outweighs American education until the achievement gap becomes a convenient exploitation or unavoidable trap door on the campaign trail. Education isn't typically a priority among elected officials until re-election time. Degenerate gamblers when it comes to education, politicians across partisan lines eagerly manipulate the education crisis when the children become the nucleus of our future again in political rhetoric.

Allow me to provide a cursory history of American education reform since it began in 1965 to better help you understand my story as it unfolds. The Elementary and Secondary Education Act (ESEA), signed into law by President Lyndon B. Johnson in 1965, was a part of his War on Poverty. President Johnson's legislative goal was to increase educational equity among low-income students through federal funding. Federal funding played a vital role in increasing educational equity because it offset local property tax shortfalls in disadvantaged communities.

Johnson's 1965 legislation has been reauthorized multiple times during various presidential administrations with subsequent additions and revisions. President William Clinton reauthorized ESEA through the Improving America's Schools Act of 1994. Highlights of the Clinton additions include increased assistance for disadvantaged students through Title I funding and an expanded Title V program for equity. Clinton also emphasized standards for teacher preparation and certification standards and an implementation of national education technology training. I earned postgraduate professional teaching credentials in 1994 that prepared me well to deliver instruction and implement classroom management strategies. As a public school teacher, I received the educational technology training by Clinton's legislation that further enhanced my ability to present lessons and maintain data. I also witnessed the implementation of the safe, drug-free school policies that federally protected school grounds to keep our students safer.

President George. W. Bush reauthorized ESEA with his No Child Left Behind (NCLB) legislation in 2002. The scope of NCLB was quite ambitious and qualitative in terms of student performance data. The Bush reauthorization legally mandated a 100% both in proficiency rating for every American child in twelve years with a deadline of 2014. Each state determined its own proficiency ratings and selected its own end of year assessments. Bush's reauthorization, like Clinton's, required professional certification for all instructional personnel in every school. The Clinton and Bush reauthorizations became game changers for all children because their initiatives recognized the correlation between increasing academic achievement and the quality of teacher and administrator preparation.

In 2009, President Barack Obama reauthorized ESEA as a part of the American Recovery and Reinvestment Act with the Race To The Top initiative. Race To The Top is a group of grants nineteen states received based on their agreement to comply with new federal testing and teaching requirements. Race To The Top became a part of the advent of the Common Core, the academic standards and goals various governors and state educators developed. It is noteworthy that the Common Core was not a part of NCLB. It is the result of collaboration among Race To The Top grant recipients.

Unique Obama changes include multiple components. First, conditional waivers were permitted for states to avoid compliance to NCLB. These waivers, as did NCLB, placed heavier financial burdens on state education departments and local school systems. Varying from the Clinton and Bush emphasis on professional preparation and credentials for instructional personnel, Obama's reauthorization focused more on principal and teacher effectiveness than preparation. Professional effectiveness is definitely a crucial skill instructional personnel must have. However, it's difficult to be effective if you're not properly prepared to teach or lead.

  The Obama reauthorization also added an additional layer of state accountability systems and more frequent academic student testing. The two most injurious outcomes of the Obama reauthorization are the deeper cheating scandals that rocked many urban areas and the less stringent standards by which some teachers, school based administrators and superintendents/chancellors have been prepared and hired to serve our children. Merit pay, bonuses and the pressure exerted toward teachers and school based administrators to increase student achievement during interval testing in concert with lower teacher preparation standards has resulted in the unprecedented cheating scandals that rocked the nation. Two prime examples, the Atlanta Public Schools (APS) and District of Columbia Public Schools (DCPS), come to mind.

  Various educators in APS received prison sentences in one of the largest cheating scandals in American educational history. News of the DCPS cheating scandal, one of the most comprehensive cheating incidents broke in USA Today with an unprecedented number of wrong-to-right erasures. Interestingly, officials for the State of Georgia took the cheating scandal seriously. Many people didn't understand why law enforcement became involved. Law enforcement became involved because there was a conspiracy to cheat. Many employees were coerced to cheat and conceal truthful scores with wrong to right erasures. Some school system employees falsely claimed federal funding as merit pay and incentives for scores they did not earn. The larger scandal that unfolded in the nation's capitol, a city that is federally funded and under the supervision of Congress, remains insufficiently investigated and unresolved, although the same issues with cheating and use of federal funds for merit pay and incentives are involved.

One other significant change occurred as a result of the Obama changes, the increase in alternative teacher, administrator and superintendent preparation programs. The three most prominent alternative education preparation programs are Teach For America, New Leaders for New Schools and The Broad Academy. Teach For America (TFA) endeavors as an organization to prepare public school teachers. TFA shares on its website that they've helped prepare more than 50,000 teachers to work with American students. There are three requirements for consideration to become a TFA Fellow – a bachelor's degree, a 2.5 grade point average and American citizenship. Exceptions to the grade point average are detailed on the website. TFA candidates who earned a lower grade point average are permitted only to teach in the DC metropolitan area, Colorado, the Las Vegas Valley, Milwaukee, Phoenix and Oklahoma. No explanation is provided about exceptions are made for Fellows to work with these students rather than being placed with all students.

TFA Fellows receive teacher training during a summer institute that includes a five-day regional induction, a five to seven week teaching residency where they teacher summer school and a subsequent orientation. This five to seven week institute provides their knowledge and skills base and mindset for teaching. In contrast, teachers who are traditionally prepared through accredited university programs as required by the Clinton and Bush reauthorizations, complete at least eighteen hours of coursework and a semester-long student teaching program. During student teaching, teacher certification candidates benefit from coaching, continuous observations and evaluations with cooperating teachers and an assigned university professor.

New Leaders for New Schools, (NLNS), another educational start-up, focuses on developing school-based administrators. Founded in 2000, NLNS website states that the organization develops "transformative school leaders" and that they "design effective leadership policies and practices for school systems across the country." NLNS conducts a year-long on the job residency for each participant. Some of the participants NLNS chooses to transform into public school administrators do not have teaching experience and are introduced to educational leadership careers from diverse industries. It is possible for a person to leave the car sales profession and become a public school principal after completing a brief program. During an on the job residency, program participants lead a school team, serve on the school's Instructional Leadership Team and lead a mandate to increase test scores. Hubs for NLNS include but are not limited to California's Bay Area and Los Angeles, Charlotte-Mecklenburg, Greater New Orleans, Baltimore and Prince George's County Maryland, Memphis, Milwaukee, New York City, Newark and the District of Columbia.

In contrast, traditionally prepared educational administrators as required by the Clinton and Bush reauthorizations attend at least eighteen hours of graduate coursework and complete an administrative internship that includes coaching, continuous observation and evaluations and an assigned university professor. After successfully completing this postgraduate professional certification and earning a passing score on the School Licensure Leadership Assessment (SLLA), administrative candidates become certified by the state where they are hired to work with teachers, students and their parents in local school systems. These traditionally prepared administrators are experienced teachers prior to becoming administrative candidates.

The Broad Academy, another private organization, describes its purpose on their website as providing knowledge and training for their hand-selected superintendent candidates on improvement strategies, equity and transformational leadership skills. The Academy also shares that they develop personalized plans for each participant and they pride themselves on the network of superintendents they create among their superintendents. Broad Academy participants attend five sessions of coursework over a two-year period along with completing monthly activities. Participants, some of whom have not been educators, are placed in key leadership positions in school systems across the country once they complete the program. More than 160 Broad participants have completed the academy and have worked in, among others, Houston, New York City, the District of Columbia, Los Angeles, Baltimore and Prince George's County Maryland, and Charlotte-Mecklenburg.

Comparatively, traditionally prepared superintendents build on their prior education and experience as educational administrators and teachers by completing at least fifteen hours of coursework, a minimum one semester internship with a certified superintendent and designated university professor. The final step is completing a professional certification assessment to obtain professional licensure.

Consider this analogy. If your spouse, child, parent or sibling suffered a catastrophic accident or received a diagnosis for a potentially deadly illness, would you consult with a trauma surgeon or specialist who is thoroughly prepared with a medical and specialty education, residency and experience, or would you select a physician who completed express six week training? I would choose credentials, experience and expertise and I daresay you would also choose the most thoroughly prepared medical professional.

Do our children deserve any less? I don't believe they do. Education is one of the only professions where too many people devalue experience and preparation. We don't allow physicians or attorneys to simply decide to become educators. Why do we accept shortcuts when it comes to those who educate our children?

I don't doubt these three auxiliary programs provide beneficial training. However, as an experienced, highly qualified educator, I believe these organizations would better supplement traditional education preparation programs and school system professional development than they have through their attempts at supplanting experience and preparation. More of our students would benefit from the knowledge and wider skill set educators would develop through combined resources. With supplemental programs like these becoming a significant part of the workforce among so many beleaguered school districts without producing stellar results, substantive and sustainable change must become a priority. No quick fix or stand-alone organization is the panacea for all that ails American education. We've been fighting a battle for equal educational opportunities for socioeconomically disadvantaged children since President Johnson began the War on Poverty in 1965, yet we're not advancing the front line as much as our children need us to.

The reauthorizations in the Clinton and Bush administrations were consistent in putting a dent in the achievement gap among minority students because educators fulfilled specific criteria to teach our children. Their experience benefitted the children and their colleagues. When the Obama reauthorization introduced ancillary groups as the reformers and financial incentives in large measure throughout the nineteen states that received Race To the Top incentives, educational reform suffered because knowledge and experience became a badge of shame, a place where reformers built their reputations as mavericks on the backs of those who had the knowledge, experience and passion to make a difference for children, not for a movement. One of the most divisive and damaging tactics used nationally in urban areas where students need stability the most over the past decade are school closures.

    School closures, used as tools of school improvement, cloak desperately neglected buildings and underserved students in countless urban areas despite the fact they most often add no value to reform. More often than not, school closures remove at-risk students from nurturing environments where adults who are familiar with their academic and socioeconomic needs are working closely on their behalf. When at risk students are haphazardly scattered across a school district, they lose the intervention and academic plans in place to support their needs. As a result, many students fall through the cracks and fall even further beneath the achievement gap. Tragically, these students are set up for failure because their educational needs have never been met and they learn in schools that aren't up to par.

    There are also instances in school systems across the nation where economically empowered parents have had to donate a designated amount of money per child to meet the shortfalls created by school budget allotments allocated to schools by central office administrators. This is also a poor way to educate our children and an unfair burden on parents whose tax dollars aren't being spent wisely or prioritized for the children. With the amount of money being spent on educating our children, there is no logical reason so much money is being wasted on top heavy central office administrative positions, experimental programs, testing preparation materials and professional development that isn't always tied to teaching methods or desired achievement outcomes. We are fighting a battle that began in 1965 and too many of our socioeconomically disadvantaged children remain casualties of war.

    I've provided this background on educational reform and the trends that emerged over the past decade to provide a context for my experiences as a credentialed educator. Unlike the changes that took place during the Clinton and Bush administrations, so many aspects of our schools systems have changed because of federal initiatives during the past decade in terms of funding, leadership practices and the introduction of employees who lacked the practical on the job experience needed to understand let alone impact sustainable change for our students, teachers and their principals. Just as a doctor cannot treat patients without proper training and residency, it is very difficult for novice teachers and administrators to survive and thrive if they are unprepared *and ineffective*. While school systems do have vital business functions, educating children is not a business, it is a process. So many of our schools have been left broken, some beyond repair, because too many federal changes and mandates came too quickly, sometimes with bonuses and merit pay as the only incentive with little research to prove effectiveness. Change isn't good when it isn't sustainable and change for the sake of change is almost always a bad thing.

All of these factors play prominently in what happened to me and my students, faculty, staff, parents, community partners and so many other schools around the nation. In 2008, school system officials where I was principal, leaders who happened to be nontraditionally qualified, abruptly closed the school where I served as principal. The unceremonious closure was particularly puzzling to our school community because we had just been fully funded for modernization two months earlier. The clandestine story behind our school's closure provides a clear backdrop of some of the issues that derail closing the achievement gap and making sustainable educational improvement. For the first time I'm sharing an unfettered account of the triumvirate of abuse I experienced as a public school administrator and the seven life-changing lessons I learned as a result that have created a powerful shift in my life.

As I share the pieces of my story, the shift in educational reform will make more sense to you. I have a threefold purpose for sharing my story. May it improve the lives of our children and educators. May it expose and establish our need to hold our elected officials and those our leaders appoint to leadership positions accountable and to higher standards. Third but not least, may it show there is always victory in disappointing situations when we choose to be defiant and brave enough to face our truths and share them with others for the greater good.

CHAPTER TWO:
The List

You learn something special from playing the most difficult games, the games where winning is close to impossible and losing is catastrophic. You learn how to compete as if your life depended on it.

Jay Z
Decoded

The Precipice of Change: The Renovation List

On Wednesday, September 5, 2007, the calm before my storm began unsuspectingly when I met an educational facilities consultant. Introducing herself via email, she announced our school had been scheduled and funded for a 2008 modernization. After our online conversation I smiled more brightly than a lighthouse beacon. The news thrilled me. I eagerly anticipated our first face to face meeting with complete gratitude and a renewed hope. Reflecting on our school's horrific conditions, I felt overwhelming joy and relief because our students would soon attend a modernized school that didn't look like a long abandoned building in a bomb-ravaged war zone.

The facilities consultant and I completed our first site visit a week later on September 13, 2007. During our walkthrough, the consultant seemed visibly moved by the dilapidation and disrepair she observed. We held several subsequent meetings in October. Once the School Instructional Team saw the blueprints and learned details about the amenities we would have, there were tears in my eyes and in a few of theirs as well. Each subsequent meeting with the consultant renewed our team's hopes, encouraging us to believe better times lay ahead for our school community.

Advocating for Change

The pending modernization evoked unforgettable memories. The inexcusable conditions of our school's community provided a prime opportunity during my first month as principal in 2005 to fight for change. When my appointment began, facilities struggles literally greeted me at the front door. There is a direct link between the quality of a school's facilities and student achievement. Appalled by the conditions in which my students attended school, I requested a meeting with our school's city council representative, Adrian M. Fenty, several appointed city officials and parents. I prepared a binder of every unresolved work order to present to each person during the meeting.

The repairs we discussed during the meeting highlighted serious, longstanding neglect. Most of them, safety risks and fire code violations, were several years old. For example, a man made river ran along our ground floor from the boys' restroom. The restroom ceiling collapsed for the second time in less than a year after it had been cosmetically patched. Once the ceiling collapsed a second time, rainfall pooled on the floor, it created an ideal breeding ground for mold and safety hazards. Two inoperable urinals in the restroom clogged with urine and toilet paper emanated an unforgettable funk. The inoperable urinals coupled with the collapsed ceiling and debris across the floor provided a proverbial recipe for disaster. As a result of cyclical neglect and disrepair, most of the tiles in the restroom and hallway had become laden with black mold. The moldy tiles continuously popped up as a result of pooling water. Missing floor tiles posed tripping hazards and the mold remained unabated. Shockingly, our school division had no problem with this area being used for city-sponsored after school activities in our adjoined recreation center. The other repairs we discussed included exposed electrical wires, broken safety catches on our doors, missing door handles, peeling paint and a plethora of graffiti. Most of the graffiti represented various neighborhood "crews," the police department's politically correct euphemism for gangs.

    I appreciated then Councilmember Fenty's enthusiasm and what appeared to be a commitment to advocate for completion of these direly needed repairs. Encouraged by his promises of action, I believed the repairs would be completed if only for the political accolades that would undoubtedly become the councilmember's prize. What I did not anticipate is that the work orders, a matter of public record, would so quickly become a part of the Fenty agenda to propel his political aspirations. I've never been a naive woman. Knowing all things to be political, I took the calculated risk I had to take to provide a better learning environment for my students. To his credit, Mr. Fenty exerted political pressure and, as a result, the facilities department made many repairs that at least cosmetically improved our school for the short term.

Everything Is Political

Everything in a school system is as political as matters with federal, state and local government affairs. It's simply more of a disgusting game because it affects our children. Once my supervisor's supervisor became aware of the details of my meeting, I definitely wasn't commended for going the distance to improve our facilities. During a thorough managerial tizzy, I received a tongue lashing for sharing "school system information" with a "mayoral candidate" and 'systemic outsider." Sharing the work orders and taking the group on a guided tour to see the inexcusable conditions my students had to endure each day became my last line of defense. There was little else I could do after inheriting a deplorable building and submitting multiple work orders for repairs that had been requested during the three and four years before I became the school's leader. My responsibilities, in addition to supervising instruction for students along with the adults who provided instruction to our students and many other tasks required by the central administration, included providing a facility where my students could learn and teachers could provide instruction safely and efficiently. The scolding I received was well worth the repairs made and the reputation assigned to me of being a maverick however duplicitously assigned to me became worthwhile.

  While reminiscing about these events, the modernization email became an even brighter beacon of hope for our school community. After benefitting from band-aid repairs for two years as a result of Mr. Fenty's intervention, our school community would finally receive what we actually deserved. The promised modernization meant my students would finally attend a school with facilities conducive to learning, a dream that had been long deferred to them. My teachers would finally have technologically equipped classrooms where they could provide daily instruction at 21st century standards. Our parents, many of whom attended our school as children, expressed joy about the pending renovation. They appreciated the opportunities their children would have. The modernization plans included pottery kilns, labs for art classes, piano and voice lessons and writing labs along with many other amenities. We would even have a modernized recreation center that would benefit the community at large.

  The renovation elated our custodial team too. We would finally have a new roof that wouldn't leak each time it rained or snowed as ours had for at least six years. Every time it rained, our custodians had to place large trash barrels and buckets throughout the building to catch leaking water. Only when an aftercare provider fell by the cafeteria and injured herself in a puddle and submitted an incident report did it become a priority to repair the roof for liability's sake. The other leaks? They continued leaking despite the stream of work orders we submitted for three years, not to mention the three and four years of preceding work orders.

    The roof repair wasn't the only work order the facilities department stubbornly ignored. A dual heating and air conditioning unit languished in its box under a classroom table. While the head custodian submitted countless work orders and repeatedly called facilities for assistance, the teacher and students continued to suffer in sweltering summer heat with fans or frigid winter cold with space heaters because of inaction and creative excuses about why the repair had been delayed. Some of our student restrooms had missing bottom portions of their entry doors. The missing portions, completely unacceptable, angrily reminded me of doggie doors. There was at least one inoperable urinal and toilet in each restroom. These nonfunctioning flushing systems proved to be a challenge for our custodial team to maintain clean, fresh smelling facilities. It angered me that my students received consistently substandard treatment than their more economically empowered peers attending other schools.

We Didn't Wait for the Help That Never Came

Beginning my first year as our school's principal, it was obvious the school system's central administrators lacked a commitment to increase our meager instructional and operating resources so the teachers and I, along with some of our parents, worked diligently to establish and maintain partnerships with outside funding sources. Teachers introduced strategic partners who faithfully contributed their time as tutors and mentors. Strategic partners donated equipment, books and their time for school beautification projects to provide resources we would otherwise have gone without. One particular partner I found showed a heartwarming affinity for our students. They realized how crucial it is to maintain a safe, orderly and appealing learning environment where children feel wanted and welcome. They provided hundreds of cans of paint to beautify our school and worked alongside us to paint. They replaced the broken doors that besmirched our student restrooms.

Two artists provided murals that captivated our students. I remember how the primary students squealed with delight and pure joy when they glimpsed a Finding Nemo mural and several others on the primary wing by one of our artists. An original mural of national monuments and words of welcome in each of the languages our school community spoke graced our school's foyer. Our other artist created beautiful, lifelike murals of famous Washingtonians and Black and Latino Americans for the cafeteria and he painted a map of each country our students' families had immigrated from to instill pride and unity among our families.

Another generous partner provided athletic equipment for each of our classes to use during recess. This was especially important because the annual mandatory central office funding reductions had eliminated our physical education and arts classes. As a musician and enthusiast for the performing arts, this had always been a painful budget cut for me and one for which I took a lot of abuse. Most of the faculty and staff members whose positions had been cut always blamed me, yet I couldn't appropriate positions our budget did not allot. I never made the excuses I could've made because posturing wouldn't bring those positions back. Still, the biggest loss translated yet again to our students who once again lost countless opportunities they so richly deserved.

While Rhee and her central administration leadership continued to ignore our concerns about our budgetary constraints and the sparse, inefficient internet network, one of our partners provided two reliable internet servers and two computer labs where our students had real-time access to computers for extended learning, curricular enrichment and test preparation skills. I cannot describe the joy we felt when our students finally received this baseline of the minimal resources the children in the school district's more economically empowered schools automatically had. This generous partner also provided a back pack and umbrella for *each* of our students.

    We also had a gardening partnership that provided opportunities for our students to visit farms and to have their own garden on our school grounds. The students maintained and cared for the garden and one grade level became inspired to create a flower garden. One of our teachers created a cooking club so students could have the opportunity to prepare and taste the fruits of their labor. This partner also provided a beautiful spruce tree for the holidays each year and coordinated a visit from a cow so the students could experience milking a cow and learn more about the roles cows play on a farm.

    Many of our parents and grandparents participated in beautification projects. They donated materials and money to teachers throughout the years. Our students did not miss field trips or extended learning experiences because their parents could not pay. In many ways, we became that proverbial village every American child deserves. It was the least we could do for students who deserved so much more from a school district that continuously failed them.

Dirtier Politics than Usual

Despite the three years of facilities challenges I inherited, hope burned in my heart for two months that everything would change once our modernization processes ended until I received a cavalier phone call from Kaya Henderson, the Deputy Chancellor and overseer of Human Resources for the school system. "Your school has been added to the closure list." In nine words and sixteen syllables, my career as an urban public school administrator crumbled. Until that moment, I never believed mere words could alter the trajectory of my career and my life but they did, quickly and unequivocally. After all, the message Deputy Chancellor Henderson gave me was very telling. "Your school has been added to the closure list." That means it was not a part of the original list. Those nine words and sixteen syllables had far-reaching implications and consequences for many. The six month countdown to those life-changing words becoming a reality began in November 2007, and they ravaged my spirit with the destructive ferocity of a grizzly's paws. Once the cold thirty second phone call ended, I gasped for air, struggling to maintain my composure. My world shook and then stood eerily and deathly still.

Nearly a decade later, here I stand, choosing defiantly to break my silence on my terms and extremely grateful for every lesson I've learned. I used to wonder why some people who experience difficulties caused by abuse of power, harassment and intimidation kept silent while others spoke out. I intimately understand people cannot share their stories until they're ready to face the inevitable backlash and sometimes hateful bullying they receive. After enduring and growing through my politically charged lynching, I keenly understand why it's vital to handle every situation and person differently. There is a time to speak and a time to be silent. My time to speak has come. My story is made of many pieces and all of the pieces matter. Let's put the pieces together so you'll intimately understand why my experiences matter to me and why they should matter to you.

CHAPTER THREE:
What Lies Beneath

"We're building something here, detective. We're building it from scratch. All the pieces matter."

Lester Freamon,
The Wire

Two months after holding team meetings with our facilities consultant and looking at renovation blueprints and other documents, school system officials abruptly deflated our dreams. In two months, a vapor of time, our brief exhilaration and hope became defeated, crushed spirits. Unable to comprehend such a rapid turn of events, we became perplexed, then angry. The true reason for our school's closure emerged stealthily in November.

Protect, Serve or Intimidate?

On November 19, 2007, my life took an unexpected turn onto a dark path, beginning the most grueling journey of my lifetime. The journey began when an unexpected phone call sharply punctuated my day. Sergeant J. J. McCourt, an officer assigned to the Metropolitan Police Department's Internal Affairs Division called, advising me my name had come up as a person of interest in an investigation he was working. As a law abiding citizen, my heart nearly exploded from panicked palpitations.

I fell into the chair at my desk, head spinning like a clichéd top. I immediately grabbed my journal to take private notes as he continued talking casually during what I considered an alarming, invasive phone call. When I asked him what his investigation entailed and how it involved me, the Sergeant refused to provide further information. Instead, he continued to insistently repeat it was imperative for me to comply and cooperate and that he would explain what the matter concerned when I reported to his office. The more I assured him I would not report for an interrogation without being informed what it was about, the more insistent and aggressive he became, saying he had to "wrap this matter up" for the Chief and his supervisor. At that time, Cathy L. Lanier served as police chief and Peter Newsham, the current police chief, served Lanier as one of her Deputy Chiefs. Newsham supervised Internal Affairs at the time Sgt. McCourt began harassing me.

Criminals are read their rights once they're informed why they're being arrested. I wasn't a criminal. I didn't have a hidden agenda but it became morbidly clear the police department did. Internal Affairs divisions investigate departmental issues and personnel concerns from within. I didn't know of any issues so I couldn't speak to anything official. My parents did not rear a fool. There was no way I would ever cross that blue line to discuss an undisclosed subject nor would I ever participate in any police matter without an attorney. I simply don't trust police to discuss any issue without legal representation about anything when tangled in their crosshairs. Once the phone call ended, I took a deep breath and exhaled. Unaccustomed to receiving probing phone calls from law enforcement officials about police business, I felt a roll call of emotions. Panicked. Fearful. Agitated. Dismay. Violated. Offended.

My mind reeled. I instinctively knew what he wanted to discuss and why he had taken such a deceptive tactic to summon me to his office. He couldn't approach me directly because he had a crooked agenda. I was involved in a personal relationship with a high-ranking police officer. Our friendship crossed inappropriate boundaries that included sexting and intimacy. He was married, I was not. We should never have crossed those lines – but we did. Our involvement, completely out of order, drew me into a cat and mouse game with people who wear Kevlar vests while shooting unarmed people with live fire, figuratively and literally. The ill advised, careless and selfish choices I made drew me into this gunfight. It wasn't my proudest moment but I own what I did and have learned from it.

Establishing a Pattern

Soon, I discovered how sharp and accurate my instincts had been. Obviously driven by his superiors to complete the investigation, the Sergeant called a second time that afternoon. Once again, he refused to disclose the subject of his investigation and I remained resolute not to comply with an undisclosed request. The second phone call, even more unwelcome than the first, established an emerging pattern of police harassment, intimidation and abuse of power. Acting on behalf of Internal Affairs, the division within a police department that burns its own, the Sergeant's actions and demeanor frightened me. I couldn't understand at the time why it was so imperative to harass me. I knew someone very highly positioned intended to use him to push that blue line against me by any means necessary. In that moment, I realized it was time to wear my protective vest and strap up for the coming battle. I told him I would confer with legal counsel, my figurative protective vest. After telling him I felt harassed and intimidated, I directed him to stop contacting me during my work day and from that moment forward, to contact me via my private email address. Police harassment and intimidation isn't always physical. Implied threats and mental intimidation are equally as menacing, a reality that proved itself as this Internal Affairs drama unfolded and intensified.

 My heart, frozen from the pressure, became an iceberg. A monstrous weight held me down, so much so that I ached as if the police had kicked, slapped and punched me all over my body. Mental games are often just as exhausting as taking a physical beating. Whenever we have secret compartments in our lives, we must accept the reality that our secrets could surface and potentially alter the trajectory of our lives. Next, I thought of my parents and how utterly disappointed they would be with the selfish, careless choices I'd made. My parents always set the highest expectations and, until this moment, I'd never done anything I thought would be beyond the realm of their acceptance. I felt a primal shame. What would they say? How would I explain this? The dread I felt became a millstone around my neck that picked at me, pulling me into another sunken place of fear, nervousness, despair and shame.

Can't Stop? Or Won't Stop?

Despite being advised to stop calling me the previous day, the Sergeant persisted the next day as a tightly wound soldier with orders does, calling me a third time. Playing the good cop role, he tried a new approach by disguising his call as a plea for help in the voicemail he left. In response, I emailed the Sergeant to explain I was too busy with activities at school to complete an interrogation, particularly one about a subject he refused to officially clarify. That day, through the generosity of one of our strategic partners, we gave complete turkey dinners to each family, faculty and staff member and we also had a school-wide assembly. An ever-present threat, Sgt. McCourt countered my refusal with a crafty offer to work overtime during the Thanksgiving holiday to accommodate "my schedule." I promptly informed him I would not sacrifice time with my family to speak with him about a mystery matter. There was no way I would continuously torment myself by allowing him to stalk me like prey. It was time to formally retain legal counsel.

Acquaintances, family members and friends, some of whom are police officers, have always advised me that no one should ever to speak to law enforcement with legal counsel. This makes sense. Why talk to any law enforcement official without protection since they are permitted to lie in order to obtain the information they seek? Why expose yourself to entrapment and trickery with people who are comfortable and experienced with using them interchangeably to achieve departmental goals?

Putting on My Bulletproof Vest

I intently selected Robert Greenberg, an attorney who'd earned a stellar reputation and held an outstanding trial and appellate court record. Mr. Greenberg had served as the Assistant General Counsel for the Metropolitan Police Department so he was wholly knowledgeable of their departmental policies, procedures and practices. Upon being retained, he advised me to hang up on anyone from the police department who contacted me. The day after retaining legal counsel, I received a call that significantly upped the ante of the police department's sinister cat and mouse game and the excessive force they used to force my hand.

CHAPTER FOUR:
Deeper Into the Rat Hole

"I heard, "Son, do you know why I'm stopping you for?"
'Cause I'm young and I'm black and my hat's real low?
Do I look like a mind reader, sir? I don't know.
Am I under arrest or should I guess some more?
"Well, you was doing 55 in a 54.
License and registration and step out of the car,
Are you carrying a weapon on you? I know a lot of you are."
I ain't stepping out of shit, all my paper's legit.
"Well, do you mind if I look around the car a little bit?"
Well, my glove compartment is locked,
So is the trunk in the back
And I know my rights, so you gon' need a warrant for that.
"Aren't you sharp as a tack? You some type of lawyer or something?
Somebody important or something?"
Well, I ain't passed the bar, but I know a little bit,
Enough that you won't illegally search my shit."

Jay Z
99 Problems

The Interloper

The day after I retained legal counsel, I received an intrusive call that intensified my dramatic interactions with the Sergeant. My caller, an infamous self-proclaimed community activist and "friend" to countless elected and appointed officials and some among the city's high society, audaciously called me in a feeble attempt to interrogate me. This woman, to whom I'll refer to as The Interloper, asked pointed, detailed questions only an insider within the police department's Internal Affairs division and familiar with the investigation *should* know. Familiar with the caller's capabilities, I knew The Interloper as a conniving and treacherous individual from personal experience. I listened painstakingly and placed the call on speakerphone with my administrative assistant present so she could bear witness to the conversation. I drafted an email to my attorney during the call for rapid documentation's sake.

Quite fortuitously, the caller eagerly provided every detail Sergeant McCourt concealed with glee, while disclosing the scope and focus of the investigation, the date and time I had been summoned to report for interrogation and that the Internal Affairs division had been analyzing my friend's departmentally issued cell phone and laptop. The leak within Internal Affairs and the department at large also became evident since a civilian had the chutzpah to question me as if she legitimately had the authority to do so. Though quite unwelcome, the prying phone call served me well by providing definitive proof of the department's intentions. It underscored my inherent distrust of Sergeant McCourt, Internal Affairs and in the leadership for the Metropolitan Police Department as a whole. It also proved strings had been pulled by a much higher authority than that of a desk sergeant's.

The Sound of the Police

Less than two minutes after disconnecting the call, the effrontery continued. The Sergeant doggedly called again despite my attorney explicitly directing him not to do so. When I confronted him on speakerphone in my administrative assistant's presence about The Interloper's call and pointed out the peculiar immediacy of his subsequent call, he poorly assumed the role of 'bad cop." Using a predictable reverse psychology ploy as his grand finale, one my more circumspect elementary school students would detect and rebuff, he began insisting I "come on in" to "clear your name." "Clear your name" is low-level police semantics that translates to "retain an attorney," which I'd already done. Each of his crude scare tactics clearly indicated information had been leaked through various channels to elicit information I wouldn't voluntarily provide. I refused to allow the Sergeant to coerce my compliance.

The Interloper's intrusive call and the Sergeant's subsequent opportune call created another enigma. This Interloper, a civilian, had clearly been well informed despite the fact she lacked official departmental access. Had she meddled as a result of her characteristic penchant to inject her sharp talons in other people's business or as a handler at someone else's bidding as an illicit quid pro quo? Undeniable parallels connected her illegitimate yet well-crafted questions with the scant information given to me by an audacious phone call, the matter escalated from a broadening drama to a jerry-rigged witch hunt that included a supersized combination of police harassment, intimidation and a gross invasion of my right to privacy. I became ambushed prey stalked on an open gun range with no safe haven to shield me from danger. My attorney and I concluded with swift certainty someone in ultimate authority had been single minded and cunning enough to orchestrate these shenanigans. The wagons had been circled and soon after, the ringleader emerged in the oddest of circumstances.

911 Is A Joke

From the moment The Interloper encroached on these Internal Affairs antics, my muddled thoughts became more focused because of my primal determination to survive. Imagine feeling terrorized as a police target in tandem with harassment and violation of privacy from a self-important meddling Interloper with a vile mean streak. Add to that the panic your innermost secrets will be exposed, all while being used as a pawn to harm a personal friend. On top of that, I felt intense anguish about how my actions would affect my family and friends. With that package of emotional and psychological trauma, I also experienced the intense pressure of the expectations to perform my duties consistently with excellence while under extreme duress. It was one of the most intense times in my life. Politics exist in every organization and the experiences I had would've easily escalated into an epic scandal had I not retained a skilled, master negotiator like Mr. Greenberg to represent my interests.

I lived in abject fear, visualizing the potential sensationalist headlines that could result from my selfish, reckless decision to engage in an entanglement that lacked the possibility to become anything more than a chain of stolen moments. This inappropriate relationship triggered a downward spiral that not only jeopardized the trajectory of my career but also the careers of my faculty and staff, the education of the children who attended my school, the work our strategic partners had done to supplement our meager instructional and capital resources and to bolster the socioeconomic needs of our students when the school system refused to step up to the plate. My illicit liaisons and conversations weaved a tapestry of pain and abuse . My personal business, exploited by people with their own secrets who chose to play a vicious and catty schoolyard game for diverse reasons, haunted me in the most menacing of ways.

The Interloper Had a Personal Agenda

When it came to exploitation and viciousness, The Interloper has a well-established resume that proves her adeptness to achieve the results she wants. During my first year as principal, The Interloper first emerged as an instigating troublemaker in my life. A teacher who happened to be a close friend of hers had a dispute with a parent that erupted into a shouting match of profane insults. Interrupting a school-wide assembly, our elementary students, faculty and guests witnessed an unforgettable sideshow. One of my male teachers separated both women just before the verbal spat became physical. He persuaded his colleague to leave the assembly and report to the main office. Right on her heels, the parent left too, following both teachers to the office.

Upon arriving in the office, both women began hurling insults about the other to me.

Admittedly, my first year as principal of this school introduced me to this type of raucous, inappropriate, confrontational behavior. The incident prepared me for future incidents so in that way, it proved helpful. It became hurtful among immediate events after this regrettable public display. Whenever incidents occurred, central office officials required principals to report them to our direct supervisors in case further action became necessary. When I reported this incident to my supervisor, he directed me to write a reprimand and forward it to him. He consulted with the Chief of Human Resources who subsequently issued an official reprimand along with a suspension for discourteous treatment. As you can imagine, the Chief of Human Resources' reprimand highly displeased the teacher. Ever omnipresent, The Interloper moved into position to defend the teacher, her "good girlfriend." I was amazed by how angry the teacher became when the time came to face the consequences of her actions. Instead of regretting her unprofessional behavior, she personalized the situation against me, even though her behavior created the incident.

This incident spawned a nightmare of repercussions. This teacher served as the union's building representative so she had an upper hand to use the incident to send a message to her colleagues about the reprimand and her suspension. I did not discuss it because it would have been inappropriate to discuss a confidential human resources matter. As only irony could serve, the teacher had no qualms with badmouthing me and using the incident to spread division and strife in the school. Second, for every move she could not openly make against me, The Interloper did so by proxy. From propaganda about our school's budget to the PTA and any other issue she could manipulate and exploit, The Interloper became a stalker in my professional life. During my first two years with DCPS, Dr. Clifford B. Janey, the better educated and experienced superintendent, wisely mitigated frivolous, small minded complaints. His experience provided him with the insight to recognize and deal with hidden agendas. My final year with the district became a very different experience once the system's leadership changed.

Illegal Search

The Interloper's tendency to interference and manipulate situations didn't end with me. A series of investigative newspaper articles by Jeffrey Anderson of the *Washington Times* detailed several complaints this Interloper made about Micheaux Bishop, a female police officer with the Metropolitan Police Department. The Interloper complained to then chief Cathy L. Lanier and two of her assistant police chiefs, Diane Groomes and Michael Anzallo. Her complaints led to disciplinary action against this officer and ultimately to her termination. This busy Interloper held many titles, among them former political consultant, mayoral appointee and minor elected official. She enjoyed bragging about her close ties with many current and former politicians, agency heads and the socially elite. She considered herself a personal friend to Chief Lanier, Michelle Rhee and most city council members. While reading a crime release, she noticed a familiar name among others indicted for selling various narcotics. Via email, she informed the police chief one of the alleged drug dealers in the crime release lived with one of her officers.

Her conversations with police officials about Officer Bishop didn't stop there. She divulged more of the officer's personal business in a subsequent email with two assistant police chiefs about the home the officer purchased home in July. When a departmental task force investigated Bishop, they learned she'd known this man since childhood. After reconnecting on social media, they began dating. The investigative report made several vital conclusions. First, Officer Bishop had absolutely no involvement in the alleged drug enterprise. Second, she financed her home independently through a reputable financier without any financial contributions from the alleged drug dealer. Because he was married, the Internal Affairs Division considered disciplining the officer because of the personal relationship. However, since the police department's disciplinary board hadn't penalized other personnel who had allegedly committed similar infractions, Internal Affairs cleared Bishop of wrongdoing.

Despite her role as the ringleader of the entire incident, The Interloper showed extreme displeasure and became uncharacteristically standoffish once Internal Affairs officials sought to interview her about the officer's relationship and the details she chose to share with the Chief and the two Assistant Chiefs. The Interloper threw rocks and tried to hide her hands, craftily trying to use the department to destroy her target for her. When officials first contacted her to testify in the investigation, she tried to dodge the interview. The second time officials sought to interview her, she threatened to report them to the chief. Chief Lanier's impartiality as a leader came into question after the busybody caused the firing of at least one police officer and the demotion of another.

The department dismissed the complaint against Officer Bishop in December 2009, based on a lack of evidence. In January 2010, the disciplinary board decided not to charge the officer, after which they gave her a packet of the investigation materials, including a copy of an email to Chief Lanier that identified the omnipresent Interloper as the complainant. The chief's outspoken good friend became livid because the paperwork identified her as the source. After that, the panel charged the officer with conduct unbecoming and for disclosing the witness' name. Following an evidence hearing, the panel issued a firing notice and an additional charge against Officer Bishop for lying about her personal relationship. Bishop's attorney appealed the decision with good reason because the vote to terminate her came *after* one of the department's executive leaders used "new" evidence that pushed them to change their decision.

According to Internal Affairs documents, the FBI and the police department's drug task force investigators cleared the officer as a suspect of wrongdoing and as a person of interest. The Chief's close friendship with the The Interloper as complainant became a clear conflict of interest that motivated the officer and her attorney to ask her to remove herself from the case. The situation escalated once Chief Lanier openly threatened investigative reporter Jeffrey Anderson after he revealed the facts behind the origin and nature of the complaint. So impassioned, the Chief wrote a letter to the reporter's editor criticizing its decision to publish the identity of a complaining witness and accusing Officer Bishop of disclosing confidential information. Officer Bishop had every right to face her accusers, even one who is a friend of the Chief's. The Interloper's name, recorded throughout the documenting materials and the original complaint, could not be kept confidential once it became part of a public record. During her testimony at the hearings, one of the panel members tried to help The Interloper remain anonymous once she threatened to complain to the Chief. After the request was denied, she testified in her own name as any other citizen would be required.

During her statements, other interesting facts emerged. The Interloper also knew Officer Bishop's friend. She testified about her friendship with his family, sharing how she looks at him as a brother. She also said he dealt drugs, that her son considers him an uncle and that he gave her son cash for good grades. She told investigators that she told Chief Lanier about the relationship out of loyalty to her.

According to official reports and investigative articles written by Jeffery Anderson for the *Washington Times*, a member of the department's brass, Chief demoted Inspector Victor Brito because he said the case against Officer Bishop lacked legitimate facts. Chief Lanier removed Brito as director of the disciplinary branch and demoted him from Inspector to Captain once he refused to abandon departmental rules in order to produce the outcomes Chief Lanier allegedly demanded of him. The articles drew me in. The Interloper used similar tactics while interfering with and destroying Bishop's life that she'd used against me. I wasn't the only woman who experienced her mean girl antics. In the same way she invaded my privacy and derailed my career, her actions against me became a well established pattern of behavior a year later when she shared "details" about Bishop's personal life with police brass in 2009.

30 Cops or More

Isn't it amazing how we so often fail to think of the consequences of our actions until we're facing them in unavoidable circumstances? It's human nature and one of our biggest challenges when we're entrenched in insurmountable situations. My earliest emotional doldrums began while I was in the trenches awaiting the fallout that could attack me at any moment. The curtains opened, exposing the powerful architect behind the Metropolitan Police Department's blitzkrieg. The sniper chosen to execute the bold frontal assault emerged from darkness of bushes and cover.

CHAPTER FIVE:
Pressure Points

"You want it to be one way. But it's the other way."
Marlo Stanfield
The Wire

Keyser Soze Emerges

The day after The Interloper's unwelcomed call, my administrative assistant called me to the main office for an important message. With evident concern, she told me Michelle Rhee relayed a directive to her that I should call Rhee immediately. A request of that nature typically indicates a pressing concern since the typical chain of command had been broken with a direct call. In light of the strange phone calls I'd received prior to this one, I decided to use my cellular phone. Feeling the weight of the situation, I proactively asked my administrative assistant to join the conversation so we could begin putting a plan in place to resolve the concerns being presented during the call. I used the speaker phone and instinctively decided to record the conversation. This proved to be a prudent decision as Michelle Rhee's monologue unfolded.

Rhee began the call by telling me, "Police Chief Lanier reached out to me to impress upon you the importance of participating in her departmental investigation." Continuing, she hurriedly claimed she had no idea what the investigation entailed. Her denial seemed patently absurd and sounded like a flat lie. Who would involve themselves in a fact finding mission without knowing the background facts? Whenever a typically all-knowing authority figure like Rhee hastens to convince someone they don't know to do something rash or imprudent, it's usually an indicator they're serving as a proxy or leading a fishing expedition to probe for information. When people feign ignorance, they're typically privy to more than they want their target to realize.

No Vaseline

Rhee confirmed my suspicions by asking me what the investigation entailed. I told her it concerned a personal matter in my life and that I keep my business and personal lives as separate as she did. Icily, she responded, "We all work for the same mayor and the same government." After a pause, as if for effect and because someone else was a part of the call, she continued, "The Chief told me you are not a person of interest *at this time*. You can speak to your attorney but I expect you to comply with the Chief's directive." It is impossible to understand how any reasonable adult, let alone a person in such a political position, could believe it was appropriate to act as a proxy for Chief Lanier. It's also a stretch of the imagination to fathom how any leader could believe it was acceptable or appropriate to initiate such a personally intrusive conversation with a subordinate.

A school system leader doesn't have the authority to compel an employee to comply with a coercive directive from another agency head, especially in a personal matter that had nothing to do with the employee's performance. Likewise, a sitting Chief should not have been so desperate to control the outcome of an investigation for something as seemingly trivial as cell phone and laptop usage. Such a tawdry, blatant overreach of power is unacceptable.

I remember disconnecting the call in utter disbelief. All of the pieces came together after I listened to Rhee's gangster-like diatribe of veiled threats – and believe me, every piece mattered. Rhee's cocky bull in a china shop entrance into this high-tech lynching astonished me. The Chief's surreptitiously coercive tactics and roundabout abuse of power by proxy was certainly a brazen attempt to violate my policy and to intimidate me without getting her hands dirty. The Interloper, ever the pawn, had played her role quite well too. Rhee's entrance into the fray made the situation all the more perilous. Things had become all too real.

Immediately, I recognized the ocean of potential consequences before me. No matter what decision I made, I was swimming in an ocean with relentless sharks, each determined to sharpen their fifteen rows of teeth on me for their own interests. If I participated in the interrogation, I would become a tainted pawn in a seedy chess game that didn't make sense and I would surely be disposed of as collateral damage the moment Chief Lanier decided to use me to make her next illicit move. The consequences Rhee could unleash if I publicly became the inconvenient women had drastic repercussions. I refused to continue living in a pit of anxiety each time the phone rang, wondering when the final shoe would drop. There was also the possibility The Interloper would devour me on command from the sharks who'd invited her into these choppy waters if I refused to comply. What would stop Rhee, Lanier and The Interloper from exploiting me in exchange for media sound bytes, likes and the perception of being all powerful?

I'm Not the Only One

Rhee's incident with me wasn't the Chancellor's first or only time interfering on behalf of a connected friend as an Olivia Pope-styled fixer. In one instance, while she served on the St. HOPE Board during her first term, allegations of sexual misconduct surfaced against Kevin Johnson, former professional basketball player, former mayor of Sacramento, California, now her husband. After these allegations had been reported to human resources, the Rhee spoke to human resources official Jacqueline Wong-Hernandez, assumed complete control of the situation, making sure things were "taken care of." The incident subsequently dissipated and Ms. Wong-Hernandez resigned, citing Rhee's actions as her reason for separating from the organization.

Rhee's interventions as a fixer didn't stop there. A year after I believe she punitively authorized my school for closure in retaliation for not complying with her unwise directive, Rhee scandalously assumed Olivia Pope's role again. Rhee reached out twice to Gerald Walpin, a federal Inspector General, on Johnson's behalf while his organization was under investigation to determine how the investigation was proceeding. She'd allegedly planned to give Johnson's organization lucrative contract to manage some of the District's most beleaguered high schools. When her phone call did not garner enough information about the investigation, Rhee personally visited Inspector General Walpin to vouch for Johnson's accomplishments and assure the investigator what a wonderful man Johnson was.

Rhee's penchant for interfering on her friends' behalf should not be taken lightly. It takes brazenness to breach an open federal investigation. Since she believed her actions to be appropriate to protect Johnson, now her husband, it not only begs the question why she would attempt to compel me to sandbag someone I cared about but it also amplifies her thirst for power and recklessness when aiming at targets.

In a matter of moments, I'd become intimately familiar with how it felt to be coerced by a power hungry supervisor. I'd experienced sustained police abuse of power, intimidation and harassment. I didn't savor the experience. Overnight, my life became a cheap police procedural drama about how a corrupt, petty Chief will behave with the proper motivation. I'd been overexposed to the politics of Internal Affairs and how law enforcement officials often seek to prove the conclusion they need or prefer for a particular outcome. I intimately experienced how powerful people take a situation and create the entrapping outcome they wanted. It made me wonder how many officers within the Metropolitan Police Department and citizens had been similarly mistreated and used as pawns on a chessboard. I wondered if anyone in Washington, DC, had been as physically harmed as I had been emotionally and psychologically traumatized. I began questioning whether I was physically safe while suffering this emotional nightmare.

Silence Has Repercussions

The lack of police support Rudolph Elementary School received once I refused to be Chief Lanier's snitch hardly seemed coincidental. Two specific incidents of many come to mind. The first incident occurred when a student hid in the bathroom to smoke a joint he smuggled into the building. Two teachers, the security guard and I stood aside the restroom door until the student exited and ultimately surrendered the unfinished joint from his boot. As any reasonable person would, I called the police since the law had been broken. Two school resource officers finally sauntered into the building but they did not make an arrest nor did they write a formal report. I had to negotiate with and beg the officers to remove the remaining portion of the joint from the school.

Twice these officers walked past the red and white drug free zone signs posted in front of the school. Their cavalier attitudes about the situation sickened me. Police officers should be concerned about elementary school children who are brazen enough to smoke an illegal substance in a school bathroom without the fear of repercussion. Essentially, these officers allowed this student to get high, break federal law and by implication sent a message to other children that they could do the same or worse things and get off scot free.

A similar incident occurred during the same month at a colleague's elementary school in another part of the city. Police officers arrested a student for *possession of marijuana* after finding a hidden a stash in her bra. My student possessed and smoked in a public school restroom and the police left him high and clear without tangible consequences other than a school suspension and the munchies. The laws are the same across the school district. If the police department wouldn't consistently follow federal mandates with respect to drugs on school grounds, what message did this convey to the school community?

The second incident involved two mothers who fought in the school's main hallway. After a profanity-laced tirade, one mother struck the other across her face with her cell phone. Once the struck mother defended herself, the battle ensued. There was blood, mayhem, weave and various projectile items from both mothers' purses strewn across the floor. After these combative mothers set a poor example for the children who witnessed the brawl, patrol officers answered the 911 call more quickly than the school resource officers. As the patrol officers began to secure and transfer both women to the precinct, the same school resource officers who failed to handle the marijuana incident lackadaisically strolled in. Rather than following standard operating procedure as the patrol officers were about to, one of the school resource officers took control. His brilliant solution was to suggest and require each mother to write the other a note in which they promised never to fight again at school. In addition to being a useless idea from an experienced police officer, it was another example of failure to police while sending a futile message, this time that it's alright for adults to fight and violently disturb the peace in a public school. By coincidence, the mother who initiated the altercation died nearly a month later in highly questionable circumstances while in police custody at the Fourth District. Officers responded to her home after a call of alleged violence.

There are myriad other incidents, though the two I've shared are among the most colorful. These matters lead to critical questions. Why did uniformed officers ignore serious incidents when they'd been specifically trained to respond as school safety officers? They overlooked the fact that schools are mandatory drug free zones per federal law, a law police officers are supposed to uphold. Police officers are supposed to maintain safe and orderly environments at all times. Did the officers ignore these and other incidents because I wouldn't play the snitching game? If not, there is a bigger concern. If their failure to act didn't stem from vengeance, it must have been the product of lazy law enforcement with an inconsistent application of best practices, policies and procedures with leadership that didn't focus on departmental priorities.

Crooked Officer?

Chief Lanier's actions, intended to intimidate and coerce me, piqued my curiosity. The inaction of her designated school resource officers drew more attention as well. Why call in a personal favor of such magnitude and risk exposure over an administrative hearing? According to the language used in the department's general orders, misusing one's official position and unlawfully coercing someone for personal gain or benefit violates departmental policies and procedures. Police officers take an oath to follow departmental guidelines, serve the community, protect citizens and their property, protect people from deception and prevent the weak from oppression and intimidation. My encounter with Lanier demonstrates her deliberate decision to disregard the department's guidelines and conspiracy to involve civilians in helping her circumvent policy. How could she hold anyone else accountable as a leader when her personal actions set such a poor example? The Chief chose to contact my highest supervisor, dodging my legal counsel after he previously advised the Sergeant to communicate through him. This demonstrates a blatant and calculated disregard for my privacy and rights. To what end?

Just A Friendly Game of Baseball

After reading Jay Z's book *Decoded*, his account of the evening he performed *Can I Get A* with Ja Rule at a club and encounter with the police gripped me. Once he left the performance, Jay Z recalled a police surveillance van cutting his vehicle off abruptly. At the end of the incident, laced with police movement and hysteria, officers forcibly removed Jay Z from his vehicle and loaded him into an NYPD cruiser. Just before being placed in the police car, one of the officers called someone to proudly announce he "got Jay Z." Afterward, his partner arrested Jay Z. Upon arriving at the precinct, Jay Z saw a board of rappers, just like the ones we see on so many police procedurals depicting criminal organizations. Seeing these boards made it clear to him that rappers had become targets that law enforcement stalked and monitored.

In the same way, I felt stalked, used as a means to an end, as if I was involved in criminal activity and could serve as an informant. Police department employees had information about me and shared it with at least one civilian. In 2007, one of the most destructive and expensive movements in American educational reform began. Just as Jay Z felt rappers had become an NYPD target, it became open season on thousands of traditionally prepared educators across the country. So many of us, thrown out like babies with the bath water, became unwilling martyrs for a pointless reform built on our backs. My experience was even more volatile because of the added police threats and pressure.

The Chief used me as a pawn in an endgame all her own. She wanted the game to end one way but it ended another way. This experience temporarily shattered me into billions of shards of glass. I could no longer believe every police officer wanted to protect and serve after this series of encounters. I'd never seen the pernicious capabilities this chief had among any other police personnel and though it's a naïve notion in hindsight, I never expected a Chief to be so surgical about achieving a goal at any cost. I became the focus of a high-tech lynching and my personal life became departmental fodder because of the Chief's overzealous desire to achieve her goal, making me the inconvenient woman in an avoidable situation she created. The question I continue asking is why Lanier felt compelled to act as she did. By whom had she been pressured? Her desperate behavior had to stem from a more important agenda than delving into a personal friendship that had nothing to do with her. Who was pulling her strings? Equally as importantly, what made Rhee fold her request into a school closure?

CHAPTER SIX:
Shark Bait

"Scare up a hornet's nest, no telling who's gon' get stung."

Proposition Joe,
The Wire

As I reflect on my final turbulent year in the District of Columbia Public Schools, I realize organized confusion in a matrix of educational deform had unfolded before me. This new jack movement in the city, cloaked as a movement led by devoted reformists, started as a movement to change the face of public education at the expense of experienced educators, most of whom hadn't received the resources or support from Rhee, the one starring in the role of its savior. So much of the passionate posturing in the media disguised the baseless pillaging of people's reputations and plundering the city's students' and parents' reputations. In 2007, the events in my school system became the shot of reform heard around the world and the effects of this reform are still felt around the nation.

During my service to the District, I worked with four supervisors in three years. During the year Rhee closed my school permanently, I had two different supervisors in one academic year.

Supervisor One

I worked with my first supervisor for one month in 2005. We made great strides to improve facilities in that month that supported my students, faculty and staff until the day we closed.

Supervisor Two

My second supervisor was tough but fair. He supported me when I was right and never hesitated to pour into me to help me become a better leader. Above all else, as an ethical professional who is knowledgeable about pedagogy and content matter, he held me accountable while helping me grow and produce stronger student achievement outcomes. He never left me without his support and coaching during the academic year he supervised me, continuing to mentor me until my last day in the school system. A very direct and tactful person, he shared a wealth of knowledge as an elementary learning and teaching expert until I left the school system.

And Then There Was Number Three

Once I began working with my third supervisor, I experienced a blindsiding readjustment that left me and the school dead in the water and bait for the circling sharks. His rough, dismissive manner, likely due to his vast experience with secondary students and the contrasting inexperience with elementary schools among him and his staff created an unstable working relationship. Instead of pulling from his own challenges and growth while becoming an experienced principal, he supervised in an exacting, frosty manner. His manner made it obvious which principals he liked and which he didn't. Despite his gruff exterior and arrogant ways, I gave him the respect he deserved as my supervisor. Even though I approached the change in leadership with a positive attitude, it unfolded as one of the worst professional experiences of my life.

During our first pre-evaluation conference, he was behind schedule, so a colleague and I chatted as we each awaited our conferences. After listening to this colleague and I speak conversational Spanish, he asked if I was of Hispanic heritage. My colleague and I exchanged glances, shocked he would ask an invasive and taboo human resources question with ease. I did not want to answer the inappropriately invasive question but did so because it would have been awkward and disrespectful not to respond. Once I answered affirmatively that I was Afro-Latina, the pointedly adverse treatment began.

Quite rough around the edges, he was overtly nasty and it became increasingly difficult to work with him. Realizing things had to change, I gave him a gift on Boss's Day. When I presented him with the gift, I asked him why he was so vicious toward me and what I could do to establish a better working relationship with him for the benefit of the school community. Dumbfounded, he stared at me silently before speaking. He softened for a short time but quickly returned to his insufferable ways.

Multiple times, I made requests for instructional programming and implementation support he either ignored or challenged. One example involved a teacher's classroom assignment. Our school community, a small one, offered two classes per grade level. On my Head Start grade level, one teacher's classroom was upstairs while the other's classroom was isolated in the basement. I set the expectation for the teachers to work together and teach the children in groups according to ability. Thus, I directed the teacher in the basement to move upstairs to a vacant room next to the other. The teacher did not want to move upstairs to collaborate with her colleague so she launched a campaign among her students' parents to keep her desired classroom. When the parents complained at her coordination and request, he ordered me to move the teacher back to the original classroom. I explained to him how the classroom move would provide time for the teachers to work together and combine resources. I also tried to enlighten him that the move would repair an inequity in resources for one of the two teachers and her students. Fluid classroom instruction was obviously not one of his instructional priorities as an instructional superintendent. Obstinately, he told me that "none of my classrooms were acceptable for use," though he did nothing to support me in improving our facilities, and that what I wanted to do instructionally was "too bad." Finally, he forced me to "move the teacher as I've ordered you to." Consequently, in the midst of preparing the school for the entire faculty, staff and students, the custodial staff had to move a classroom twice to uphold an instructionally unsound decision, an edict he made ultimately to spite me in favor of a dissenting teacher while yielding to frivolous parent concerns driven by a spoiled teacher inciting unnecessary problems.

In another instance, I requested instructional support for our students and faculty and staff during the budget process while the School Improvement Team and I developed our school budget for the following year. The school district held back a percentage of each school's funding allocations at the beginning of each budgeting cycle. Our school's team wanted to use our holdback monies to boost enrollment by adding an additional Head Start classroom. In addition to boosting enrollment, this would also provide the opportunity to serve our student population with earlier academic opportunities that would help us close the achievement gap. Other principals received permission to use their holdback monies while my students, faculty and staff had that permission denied. He flatly lied in an email to me and the team's chairperson, saying it was not in his authority to grant access to the funding. We were incensed because within the same email requesting access to the funds, the school system's budget official at that time said using the money at that time was in fact my supervisor's final decision. When the team and I reviewed the emails together, it baffled us that he hadn't reviewed the entire email before responding to our request.

Another example of harassment occurred when he directed me to stop the security officer from asking him to sign in when he entered our school building, a system-wide requirement and critical part of the security officer's job. He said nastily "I'm the Superintendent and everyone knows who I am. Just like the other central office administrators, city council members and mayor don't have to sign in, neither do I. These jokes were last year's jokes." I expected him to follow the standard, established School Security policies and protocol he enforced as a central office administrator, yet he became arrogantly combative in his refusal to do so. In addition to feeling he was above safety protocols and procedures, he was also deliberately nasty more often than not. He directed me to inform both of my administrative assistants they could not share the principal's driveway anymore because it was not "aesthetically appealing" and was against Office of Facilities and Maintenance policies. Prior to this particular edict, the Building Services manager at the time told me our supervisor was planning to make this directive.

When I called the Office of Facilities and Maintenance to ask if this was a true policy of DC Public Schools, the assistant to the Director of the Office of Facilities and Maintenance informed me there was no such official policy. It was another of his many personal missions to degrade and humiliate me as a leader.

There were times he followed school security policies and procedures to the letter. In March 2007, he violated my collective bargaining rights by placing me under investigation for a bogus corporal punishment charge. Unfortunately, I was unaware of the bogus charge until the school security investigator visited the school to officially question me about the alleged incident. Once the investigator reviewed the email and spoke to the parent who supposedly sent it, the investigator quickly determined the incident and the email were bogus, after which she promptly informed my supervisor his actions violated my collective bargaining rights. When the investigator wanted to officially trace the email's origins to see who had used a parent's name to file a phony complaint, he refused to cooperate with her. In doing our own research about the incident, the investigator and I determined one of the teachers used a computer at the school to create a dummy account to play the role of a "complaining parent" because he was angry I followed systemic policy and procedure when he had been investigated after a corporal punishment allegation against him surfaced.

Naturally, as corporal punishment allegations were serious, I became hysterical when the investigator left. Soon after she left, I received a call from my supervisor. When I told him I was physically ill and needed to go to my cardiologist's office for treatment for the angina attack his actions caused, he denied my request for leave to seek medical treatment. Summoning me to his office, he offered a forced apology for his actions, claiming to have "forgotten" to notify me of the complaint. Although I realized he followed proper policy and procedure in notifying school security, he did not follow protocol and inform me until he commanded me to report to his office *after* the investigator informed me of the concern. Only then did I receive notification and a copy of the bogus email.

Perhaps his most inconsiderate, boorish act toward me occurred when he forced me to manually move dirt from one part of the schoolyard to our garden. One of our teachers received a donated truckload of dirt for our school garden. The truck dumped the dirt at an area beside the garden. An overly persistent community member who had badgered every principal within the last twenty years about the garden happened to be an old friend of the supervisor's late father.

At his height of frustration with me about this community member, the supervisor quipped that I should just treat him as if he was my grandfather. After thinking to myself he had to be insane to ask me to do this, he told me the community member had been to his office again and that I had "better have all of the dirt removed before close of business the next day." Much to my father's chagrin, as well as that of my PTA president, male teachers and business partners, I reported to school the next day and moved dirt with a shovel and wheelbarrow from 9:00 until 1:30. One of my teachers, appalled at the unreasonable directive, helped me move the dirt. The PTA president, another PTA officer and a grandmother also helped me. When I introduced my supervisor to one of the parents who helped me, he lacked the decency to say thank you. Instead, he asked the parent volunteers why we didn't move *all* of the dirt. I took pictures during the dirt digging to document the experience because it was unbelievable even as I experienced it in real time.

Numerous other instances detracted from the time and energy that would have been better spent working collaboratively to improve student achievement and facilities for the children. He blindsided me with unnecessary conferences in the middle of the day that took away time from instructional monitoring. He deliberately fell asleep during a presentation I gave during a regional meeting at his request.

It is impossible to make expected academic strides, lobby for vital repairs for your building and engage with parents when you have to work with an individual determined to play power and political games. Because I knew my efforts and goals would be more supported and my faculty, staff and students would benefit greatly by working with my former supervisor, I sent Michelle Rhee an email requesting a transfer back to my second supervisor's leadership.

I explained I felt uncomfortable making the request at our meeting the day before because my supervisor was present. I asked for the school to be reassigned to my former supervisor because we practiced similar leadership styles and believed in three guiding principles: consensus, collaboration and no-fault. His principals worked as a professional learning where community and collaboration was encouraged and celebrated. He managed his principals professionally and collaboratively with instruction as the primary focus.

I also requested the change because my custodial staff performed better with the previous supervisor. The support they received from the region's central office facilities team motivated them much more effectively than the criticism and harshness my supervisor dealt. When they had questions or concerns, the facilities supervisors were immediately available for concerns and support. The chancellor responded that she needed to talk my request through with a few people and let me know how she would move forward.

My attempt to make a positive change in supervision for my school community ruffled and rearranged his feathers when the chancellor shared my request. While my former supervisor agreed to work with me again, my current supervisor tried to persuade him to refuse. He never acknowledged the message I sent and he never forgot about it either. I never received a response from Rhee because she transferred most of the district's principals to new supervisors in late October of 2007, after the school year began and a month after our school's fateful renovation funding and approval had been announced.

The Fourth of Four

On October 29, 2007, most principals received an official email that the structure of our regions would change. Consequently, most of us received new supervisors, despite the fact that the language of our collective bargaining agreement required that the designated regional assistant superintendent must serve as supervisor for ninety days before he or she can evaluate the subordinate. Like many of my colleagues, I had been transferred and began working for my fourth supervisor, this time an older woman who retired from another school district and received an appointment to work for Rhee. This happy ending to a horrible experience pleasantly surprised me. In the beginning, we had a positive working relationship, a vast improvement from my previous year. She rarely communicated with me. Unlike most other principals, I never had a formal Site Visit with the instructional team the year I worked with my fourth and final supervisors, one of the main instruments used in our principal evaluations. My first evaluation pre-conference was uneventful as was my mid-year evaluation, although both of these conferences took place after the timeline established in our contract.

By November 2007, I was relieved I no longer had to work with my last supervisor, though he hadn't ended his dealings with me and presented a parting gift with echoing consequences. One of my colleagues was in conference with him when this former supervisor stopped to take a phone call. During that time, my colleague perceived someone had called from the police department. When the phone call ended, he told my colleague he would never believe what the call was about and proceeded to divulge that his call was about my being called into Internal Affairs to answer questions about a personal relationship with a member of the department. He asked my colleague if the member of the department in question was a relative of his, to which the colleague answered no. In the presence of my colleague, he also contacted Deputy Chancellor Kaya Henderson to make her privy to the conversation as well.

This was another completely unacceptable invasion of my privacy both on the part of my former supervisor to share the information with one of my colleagues and of Internal Affairs to further violate my privacy. It was another illegal, inappropriate attempt to coerce my compliance. My colleague, shocked information of this nature had been divulged, respected me enough to let me know. Naturally, vindictive coward he was, my former supervisor never provided *me* with the courtesy or respect of making me aware of this conversation about my personal life. I've never forgotten my colleague's forthright decision to inform me of this unfortunate turn of events.

Apparently, Deputy Chancellor Henderson took her conversation with my former supervisor seriously because on Tuesday, November 27, 2007, I received one of several phone calls and emails from then Chief of Schools Tracy Martin, and renewed efforts from the busybody community activist to dig into my life. There was a mention of the omnipresent Interloper going to the media because Martin asked what she needed to say during media coverage of the matter. I explained the situation as one about my personal life, time outside of my working hours, and therefore out of DCPS' purview, revealing no other details. After I received a second phone call from the Chief of Schools, my attorney addressed her and the phone calls from central office administrators finally stopped.

In November 2007, my supervisor called because The Interloper called her after speaking to the Chief of Schools. During this conversation, I explained once again that the matter dealt with my personal life, events that took place outside of my working hours. At the time, she responded that we all have private lives that should not interfere with our professional lives and wrote the incident off as irrelevant to my work performance. To her credit, she never mentioned the conversation again but the matter did not end there.

This fourth and final supervisor visited me twice during my final months in the school system between November and May 1st. During the first visit in November, we had a conversation with our region's school improvement specialist. When my opinion didn't mesh with hers, she abruptly told me, "I've been doing this a little longer than you so I think I know what I'm talking about." Once we were alone again, the school improvement officer advised me not to disagree with our supervisor and to listen quietly to her rants because it would not do any good to say or do anything else. Reflecting on the supervisor's deportment and the experiences other colleagues had shared with me, I took the school improvement officer at her word. This was my first time experiencing the volatile behavior so many other people had described in great detail when they had been her target.

Aside from principal's meetings, generally infomercials about things she had allegedly done as a principal in her previous district, included visits from her former staff members. I rarely communicated with my fourth supervisor unless it was through email, if a report was due or when it was necessary. On March 13th, she told me during a heated phone conversation that my previous supervisor had been emailing and discussing me with her. True to form, she spoke to me quite sharply so I didn't engage with her. There is no way to communicate reasonably with an irate person who's committed to misunderstanding you while flexing their authority. When I disconnected the call, I thought the issue was settled. She would not forward the email from my stalker former supervisor but she finally faxed a copy after three requests.

Our final conversation at school took place on March 14th during a most memorable, unannounced visit. Her manner suggested a covert agenda. Members of the staff told me she was rude and abrupt from the moment she arrived. During this unannounced visit, she became irate with me because she encountered me as I concluded a parent conference in the main office. When I attempted to clarify why I'd been in the office with the parent, she snapped at me in front of the office staff that the parent's needs did not matter at the time because I should've been in the hallways with the children. I didn't attempt to explain our discussion was about this parent's child and a sexual harassment incident. I met with the parent early and alone because she had volatile tendencies and had been barred from the school. My last supervisor prematurely lifted the bar against the parent after demeaning the parent to me as nothing more than "a deep ghetto 'bout it 'bout it girl" with whom he did not want to deal. This became yet another incident of abuse of power where my students and school's needs became a bargaining chip much less significant than his bruised ego.

    While visiting the school, she publicly berated one of my first grade teachers in her classroom, discussing the teacher in a vile, condescending manner *with the children.* Clearly intent upon humiliating this teacher, she purred cattily, "Hope she got my message," as she stormed out of the classroom. Humiliated for the teacher and the blistering scene I witnessed, I left the room behind her. Next, she berated me in front of the school nurse and a parent who was in the infirmary about an accidental injury his son suffered the afternoon before. Unfortunately, the child had been burned by a hot radiator. I spoke to the parent in Spanish so my supervisor's angry tirade would end. The parent, calm and understanding, peacefully spoke with me about the situation. My supervisor, on the other hand, called the deputy for school operations from her cellular phone, loudly proclaiming, "This parent has a lawsuit."

It was an oddly unprofessional reaction for an instructional superintendent to indicate that a parent had a potential lawsuit with such disregard for the school's interests. Matters should be thoroughly investigated before making premature conclusions, particularly in situations of financial liability. Her hostility continuously escalated as she took me into the hallway, pressing me dogmatically. Before I could answer any of her questions, she would bombard me with another one. Among some of the questions she asked me were "Had I been a teacher before?", "Had I put in any work orders?" and "Had I put in work orders for radiator covers?" In order to deescalate the situation, I suggested that we discuss these matters in my office. Fortunately, she agreed.

After this display of unprofessional behavior, I didn't feel safe with her behind closed doors. Once we sat down in my office, her hostility became uncontainable. She cursed at me several times. After calling me a "fucked up principal," she snapped, "Your school looks like shit." I tried to be as calm and professional as possible, reminding myself that it took two to argue. Whenever I tried to speak to my position, she further berated me, telling me "You're just giving me excuses." I wondered how anyone could communicate with a woman who behaved in as unruly a manner as she did. It surprised me Rhee would appoint a person who acted as unprofessionally as she did as one of her executive leaders, especially since Rhee spent the majority of her first year as chancellor berating and ridiculing her workforce. As she continued to express her displeasure, her comments made it apparent she and my former supervisor had been discussing me. Several teachers and the PTA president told me my former supervisor had accompanied her to the building that day. At that point, it became clear they decided to visit the school that day in an ambush, she as my supervisor and my former supervisor as her witness.

I tried to warn her that he had a grudge against me. Using his first name, she continuously repeated, "He wouldn't lie." It appears she listened to him without forming her own opinion of me, most likely the truth since she had not visited my school a sufficient amount of times to draw her own conclusions. She further stuck her foot in her mouth by telling me that she never thought I was "one of those schools she had to worry about," divulging this as the reason she had not visited more often. In the process, she viciously berated three other principals, detailing her opinion of their "subpar" performances. During this portion of her angry outburst, her comments became particularly painful because, unknown to her, she attacked my sorority sister and dear friend's professional performance, rebuking her as an "inept, 'bougie' debutante."

Also in March 2008, my fourth supervisor held a cluster meeting with her principals and regional staff. At the end of the meeting, she excused everyone from the room except principals and select regional staff members. As soon as the room cleared, she informed us of a series of meetings Michelle Rhee held with area superintendents and key people from her executive staff. These meetings, held to finalize decisions about who would be removed from their positions as principals, had concluded and final decisions had been made. She also disclosed that while she tried to intervene for some of us, irrevocable decisions had been made and approved by Rhee. These disclosures cast the "firings" in a unique light. Several questions can't be ignored. First, since decisions had been firm enough for my supervisor to share them with our region in March, why wait until May to ambush principals? Second and far more curiously, since these premature "firings" were irrevocable, what substantive data bolstered the premature firing decisions? It certainly wasn't test scores. This meeting became the first in a trail of bread crumbs leading to the endgame

At the beginning of her first year as Chancellor, Rhee held a fifteen minute sit-down with each principal. In most cases, their area superintendent attended the meeting too. Each of these very brief meetings focused on end of year test scores and a mandated increase by any means necessary. At the end of the cursory meetings, each principal received a summary of their meetings. Without test scores in hand, subjective decisions to terminate some principals while retaining others created the myth of educational reform and solidified Rhee's position as an educational reform movement's guru. Her unprecedented actions were nothing more than a smokescreen like the one concealing The Wizard on the *Wizard of Oz*. The Chancellor misrepresented arbitrary non-renewals as firings to gain favor in the press, using them to create a momentum she alleged led to school improvement.

Contractual Issues

In 2007, Rhee, her Deputy Chancellor Kaya Henderson and John Davis, another central office executive Rhee appointed, altered the official evaluation timelines for principals and assistant principals that had been agreed upon in the collective bargaining agreement between the administrators union, the school system and the Government of the District of Columbia. Rhee and Henderson subsequently released a document entitled "07/08 Principal Evaluation Indicators and Timelines, Final Template," on September 7, 2007. Their revisions rendered the following document:

Evaluation Timeline

Friday, September 28, 2007 – by this date, all principals will have reviewed their plans during an **initial conference** with the Regional Superintendent and/or the Chancellor.

Friday, November 9, 2007 – by this date, all principals will have a **quality review** with the Regional Superintendent and/or the Chancellor.

Friday, February 1, 2008 – by this date, all principals will have a **mid-year quality review** with the Regional Superintendent and/or the Chancellor.

Friday, June 27, 2008 – by this date, all principals will have their **end of year conference** with the Regional Superintendent and/or the Chancellor.

Thursday, July 3, 2008 – All principal evaluations will be completed.

There are key differences between the legally binding collective bargaining agreement and the 2007 modifications. The most significant differences are that the deadline for being placed on an improvement plan and the official notification for non-renewal are conspicuously absent. This revision led to multiple consequences for administrators. The revision sends the message that improvement plans have no merit. Without an improvement plan, even as subjective as they can be, how would an employee know how he or she needs to improve? How would an employee receive coaching and feedback? Without a deadline to complete improvement plans, the official notification for non-renewal from the human resources department becomes all the more crucial. Yet, this step was also removed.

The changes Rhee and her designees made vary significantly from the evaluation timeline approved by the administrators union and the school system in the collective bargaining agreement. This collective bargaining agreement is protected by the city's municipal regulations. This omission begs another set of questions. Did the union's president independently approve the modifications? If so, he violated the union's constitution and bylaws because he did not bring these changes before the membership for our approval. If school system leadership circumvented the union president's authority by altering the indicators and timelines without his knowledge they violated his authority, the rights of every member and the collective bargaining agreement itself. This is a critical factor because the collective bargaining agreement is agreed upon by school system and the union and referred to in the District's municipal laws.

Although the administrative contract defers to the municipal regulations, all revisions to legally binding agreements must be approved before they become official. There is another wrinkle with the revisions. On October 29, 2007, all principals received an email notification that the structure of our regions had changed. Consequently, the majority of principals received new supervisor assignments. Once the reassignments became official, that meant new evaluation conferences had to be completed. These transfers prevented the principals assigned to new supervisors from meeting the deadline imposed by Rhee for September 28, 2007, for the first evaluation conference and the November 9, 2007, quality review. Why make rules if you don't plan to enforce them?

    Another problematic aspect of the 2008 dismissals was the general ambivalence and disrespect with which Rhee treated at will employees. Circumstances indicate the school system's human resources department attacked at-will employees as a part of a national union bashing campaign because they perceived them as low-hanging fruit they could pluck off effortlessly. No group of workers in America, a democratic nation at least on its face, is devoid of rights. Termination processes are in place to release at will employees in every organization. Right to work states like Virginia and North Carolina are non-unionized but stable policies are in place to accommodate employee terminations within the law. That's why virtually every organization includes a termination process developed collaboratively by its personnel and legal departments for leaders to use as a guide when making employment decisions. Likewise, Rhee's administration could have legally terminated poorly performing administrators by allowing the process that worked well for her predecessors to continue rather than creating a parallel system that wasn't ethical or enforced. Moreover, Rhee and Henderson could also have designed a better process since human resources was supposedly Rhee's strong suit. If the decision to terminate employees boils down to subjective whims, why do criteria exist?

Behind the Veil of Dismissal

Virtually every principal Rhee fired faced dismal challenges. One of my colleagues, an elementary school principal in another part of the city, suffered an attempted assault when a parent leapt across her desk. He lunged at her while berating with a threatening litany of profanity. Had a security officer not been present, the parent would surely have physically attacked and severely injured my colleague. Prior to the assault, this principal requested additional security for her campus because of other violent incidents that had transpired. Even after suffering a traumatic incident with a violent parent and feeling endangered in the building personally and for the school community, no additional security personnel arrived, though the police department arrested the parent and documented the encounter.

Drunken Substitute

This colleague also dealt with a drunken substitute who, armed with a pint of E and J brandy, refused to pay cab fare upon arriving at school, choosing instead to run away from the cab driver and into the school for refuge. The police department responded to the scene and took a report from the cab driver. In accordance with human resources policy, the principal contacted her area superintendent and human resources to report the incident and prevent the substitute from working with and potentially endangering the children while intoxicated. Human resources personnel assured my colleague they would prevent the substitute from working across the school system.

A few months later, the substitute returned to my colleague for a copy of their substitute's card for payroll at another placement. According to payroll policy and procedure, if a school's payroll clerk does not have a copy of the substitute's credentials in their files, the substitute is unable to work with children. This policy is in place to ensure all substitutes are screened before they work with children. When my colleague contacted Human Resources about the matter, she was unable to persuade them why the issue was critical in terms of student safety, security and the school system's potential liabilities. Using the only strategy she had in light of the report she made, she refused to turn over a copy of the card. It appears the substitute's rights superseded student safety.

Additional Security Denied

Another of my colleagues worked in one of the most challenging secondary schools. She repeatedly asked for additional security because of her concerns about campus safety. Some security officers ordered and delivered off-campus lunches for students and collected a convenience fee for their services. Central office personnel blamed my colleague for student violence that erupted off campus. Yet, when disgruntled groups printed, distributed and posted fliers around the community with my colleague's photo captioned with 'Bark if you see this dog,' school system officials did nothing to ease the tensions of the situation nor did they extend support in light of these events. On May 5, 2008, Michelle Rhee terminated the school's entire administrative team.

Not Such A Confidential Human Resources Department

    As humiliating as the mass firings were, the insult hurled against principals did not stop there. Selected community members knew about the personnel actions before affected principals could be notified. The Interloper who stalked and attempted to interrogate me in November resurfaced when she publicized principal firings and staffing changes via email to city council members and various community members. She made this notification on Saturday, May 3, 2008, two days prior to formal notification by instructional superintendents for the affected principals on Monday, May 5. Why would and how did The Interloper once again gain access to information about personnel actions that had not yet taken place? Why would The Interloper have the access and power to disseminate emails with an open dialogue among city council and community members about supposedly confidential personnel actions?

    Too many principals deal with lack of resources, poor facilities and political melodrama among connected parents and community members. The political nature of what we do and the abuse of power we endure dilutes the energy and focus that American students deserve. The duties of a principal should first be instructional and operational as they relate to the children. faculty and staff. Yet sadly, they are not. The experiences I shared about my final year in the school district are reflective of what most urban principals experience.

**PART TWO:
ROCK BOTTOM**

"You can't start changing things in your past. Everyone has challenges and lessons to learn – we wouldn't who we are without them. I certainly wouldn't be who I am."

Sean Combs

CHAPTER SEVEN:
The Dirty South

"America ... the international Jekyll and Hyde ... the land of a thousand disguises, sneaks up on you but rarely surprises."

Gil Scott-Heron

Closure's Aftermath

Once Rudolph Elementary School closed, seeking a new administrative appointment became quite an ordeal. I didn't want to leave Rudolph because my work there wasn't done. Add to that the corrupt circumstances in which the school had been closed combined with the difficulties I encountered in moving on while Michelle Rhee continuously spoke negatively about principals whose schools she closed and who she fired, you have a perfect employment storm. The long days and evenings the faculty, staff, parents, community partners and I worked for our school community increased the amount of perseverance and determination in my leadership toolkit. We weren't a perfect community but we'd done the best we could with what we had. The deviously questionable manner in which our school had been closed left a hollow sadness within me.

Nothing about our school's closure benefitted the students or the community. Closure ripped our students from a loving community that advocated for them, had a real-time expertise about their performance and relationships with their parents and the community. Familiar with their socioeconomic needs, we wanted the best for our children. Our students' parents suddenly had to take on the burden of finding another public school for their children to attend.

Only special education students in the District of Columbia receive transportation through the school district. Without district-sponsored transportation, our students had to either walk fourteen to sixteen blocks to the closest neighborhood elementary school or they had to take public transportation if their parents did not have a car to drive them to school. Many of our students were legally too young to ride public transportation alone.

The abrupt closure affected the faculty and staff too. Some of the faculty and staff received transfers to other schools across the district while others applied for and received contracts in surrounding school districts. Others were left hanging in the wind.

New Beginning

After interviewing for a new position and being offered contracts in multiple school districts, I accepted an offer from the Charlotte Mecklenburg Public School District in Charlotte, North Carolina. The district's superintendent at that time, Dr. Peter C. Gorman, impressed me. Prior to becoming the leader of that district, Dr. Gorman served in other progressive leadership positions. His record of accomplishments initially assuaged my concerns he was a Broad alumnus. Michelle Rhee, also a Broad alumnus, completely lacked public school administrative experience and I believe her lack of experience contributed heavily to her decision to close Rudolph Elementary School so capriciously. The Broad Group, as discussed in chapter one, is an alternative, expedited approach to becoming a superintendent.

Politics As Usual

My final interview with the district prior to the offer of contract in North Carolina became a politically charged live wire. In addition to Dr. Gorman, the conversation included several of his key players – the Chief Operating Officer, Mr. Maurice Green; the Chief Academic Officer, Dr. Ruth Perez; my former supervisor, Dr. Elva Cooper, my Regional Assistant Superintendent; and, the Chief Human Resources Officer, Mr. Maurice Ambler. Dr. Gorman openly expressed his contempt for several officials affiliated with my last school district who he alleged plagiarized his and Mr. Green's Strategic Plan, a mammoth project they'd completed to drive instructional and organization goals. Still openly vexed, the Superintendent said he'd never received an apology. During this executive conversation, I stared down the barrel of the loaded gun of plagiarism. After a protracted, awkward pause, I apologized for the incident and explained that an apology was unlikely since those involved had refused to answer direct questions about it during a city council hearing convened by the District of Columbia City Council. There I was, 400 miles away from the District trying to embark on a new beginning, yet still tied to the past. I languished in my blisteringly uncomfortable seat apologizing for an incident over which I had no control.

Once I began my new position, I viewed my new opportunity through a cautiously optimistic lens. I quickly discovered the school's community functioned more as a network of social cliques than as a cohesive body. At the beginning of the leadership transition period, I remained guarded. With an uncomfortable uneasiness lingering in my spirit, my experiences from the previous year made me much less approachable and open with people than I had been before. As I adjusted to the perkiness of the South, my supervisor pulled me aside during my first week on the job to discuss a parent request to meet with me. Naturally, I was curious why a parent would want to meet with me given that I'd just come aboard. When I asked my supervisor to provide details about why this parent felt so anxious to meet with me, she said the parent was "upset and concerned" because I came to her child's school from an urban school amidst myriad blanket defamatory remarks Rhee made about countless employees in my last school system across virtually every media form. I realized her remarks about the perceived ineptitude of principals were in play four hundred miles beyond the school district.

This parent also felt "upset and alarmed" I'd worked at one of "those Title I schools with poor, urban children" and, as a result, believed I "would be unable to relate to wealthier, non-disadvantaged children with involved, two-parent households." At the time, I didn't realize this parent's attitude was pervasive among the small yet elite clique of parents who enjoyed reign of the land during the previous principal's tenure. This set of concerns, however valid to this and other likeminded parents, demeaned the achievements my students and faculty-staff had earned in the District. These poorly informed opinions based on hearsay and gossip, diminished my faculty and staff's dedication and the academic gains they earned alongside the children. These hasty conclusions also degraded my expertise in working with less economically empowered students and their families, demeaned the intelligence of people based on demographics and showed a foothold of white privilege in this school's community that soon made itself known among other parents and the faculty and staff members who associated and believed similarly. Though the conference with the parent went surprisingly well, it was foreboding of what was to come. As time passed, I realized "upset and concerned" most often represented the common state of mind among this elite group of parents when they couldn't have their way.

It concerned me when my supervisor asked me to cater to this parent. Being compelled to justify my experience and expertise became a risky precedent that emboldened other like-minded parents to encroach upon my right to privacy. It invited an undercurrent of disrespect much like the one I'd left behind. The premature parent conference and the sly maneuverings foretold what was to come. As a result of the precedent set by this the conference, I maintained private anecdotal notes on every professional conversation I had moving forward.

Open House foreshadowed more of the pettiness and other incidents of white privilege with which I would have to deal. Parents had voiced multiple concerns during the two previous years that the excessive time spent in the general PTA meeting at the beginning of the evening greatly diminished the time they could spend in the classrooms with teachers. Most of the teachers shared that some of the parents lingered long after the event ended, prolonging an already extended work day. These concerns, both valid, made sense to me. Families with two or more children needed to spend more time in classrooms than in a general PTA meeting. I decided the leadership team would accommodate the parents' wishes to spend more time in the classrooms so teachers could discuss learning and teaching and our school's current instructional goals. Any increase in time spent talking about instruction was of paramount importance to me. It also made sense to protect the teachers' time while providing a more structured event so parents would know when it was time to leave the classrooms for the evening.

During Open House, I stood by the front door throughout the entire event so I wouldn't miss the opportunity to greet each family in attendance. Imagine the endless sea of faces to greet in a compact span of time. I vividly remember at least seven parents telling me how fortunate I was to have "escaped those inner city kids" and all of their problems. It was all I could do to maintain my professionalism in light of their crude, biased comments about my previous students. Their commentary thoroughly disgusted and repulsed me while it also made me acutely aware of the negative undercurrent that existed among too many of the parents. Their ignorance of and lack of compassion toward the struggles poor children experience exasperated and saddened me. It's one thing not to understand the challenges another group faces and an entirely different matter to condemn them. Ideologically, they reminded me of the alpha wolf myth, the politically connected wolves who claim dominance and superiority to the other wolves in their packs. In truth, it was my second direct encounter with the abject white privilege alive and well in the school's community that vividly colored my professional experiences in North Carolina.

The very next day, a parent wrote the superintendent to express her dismay that I had not attended Open House. This parent's "take it to the top" attitude served as an appetizer for the main course of misplaced concerns I would be served throughout the academic year. Either this parent didn't attend the event on time or she slipped into the building through a door other than the main entrance. None of the parents who followed procedure missed meeting me.

Growing up in Virginia made me keenly aware of the dynamics unique to the South, though living in the DC metropolitan area for a decade highlighted the differences among the people in the two regions. My last student population was less diverse, much less wealthy and much less passive-aggressive. One of the differences I readily embraced when I moved to North Carolina was the opportunity to work with a more culturally diverse student population. Our world is made more beautiful and flavorful with diversity.

The faculty and staff at Rudolph Elementary School lived across the DMV, an abbreviation for the District of Columbia, Maryland and Virginia. They commuted to work and enjoyed busy lives of their own. Many of the teachers and parents in Charlotte lived closely amongst one another. The scenario was much like living in Mayberry. I expected

Aunt Bea to grab Opie by the ear at school one day for being naughty at recess. As a result of the affinity that often develops in tightly- knit communities, close relationships existed among a portion of some of the faculty and staff members and parents. Many worshipped together on Sundays. They sunbathed and tanned at community pools and shared beer and wine over homemade Carolina barbecue. There is nothing wrong with being neighborly and everyone has the right to choose their friends. However, it becomes a challenge to function professionally among intertwined hidden alliances and stealth encumbrances skulking beneath the surface. *Harvard Business Review* recommends maintaining a healthy distance between our personal and professional lives. I remember my parents teaching me similarly through the adage, "Don't mix business with pleasure."

We gain a great deal of expertise from our mistakes when we have a sense of humility. My experiences and growth as a leader provided valuable lessons about cultivating overly close relationships with previous faculties and staffs. An effective leader cannot become a part of a faction in the organization he or she leads, a lesson my experiences in Charlotte further solidified. It's essential to establish positive working relationships with the whole. In line with the Stephen Covey quote, "You can't talk your way out of a problem you behaved your way into," I set out to develop and maintain collegial relationships with each member of the school community. Although I had honorable intentions, I was unable to lead in a way that wasn't challenged at every turn by the powerful cliques in the school community, all of whom had been allowed to set the tone previously established and followed in the school during its first two years of operation. It is virtually impossible to function effectively in or be accepted in a toxic environment while battling assertive, combative power cliques.

  The previous principal was very social with selected parents and faculty-staff members, evidenced by the established social mores I encountered upon becoming the principal. A few parents could not understand why I did not want to sit on the deck with my feet up at one of the favored watering holes drinking wine and whiling the evening away. They asked why I wouldn't do what the last principal was comfortable doing. There was an overbearing familiarity and boldness among some of the adults in the school community. I received countless invitations to have cocktails and dinner with parents. Others offered tickets to professional sporting events and the use of vacation homes for weekends. Each of these invitations, however genuine they may have been, came with a delayed acceptance price and immediate burden of consequences when refused.

Winget Park Elementary School, my assigned school, is middle to upper income elementary school with a large number of students who had been identified as gifted and a small population of students living in poverty. Still, there was a significant achievement gap among the students and most of the students had not achieved at their actual potential. With that came a portion of the faculty population's deep investment in keeping things exactly as they'd traditionally been done, an attitude that made them oblivious to the need for the school to push for higher academic improvement as a team. It's difficult to grow and improve when you believe you've arrived and the destination isn't even close and that's the attitude that held the school back. Throughout the academic year I built support among faculty, staff and parents while simultaneously dousing fires set by the grumbling undercurrent.

Multiple incidents document the abundant power struggles and flagrant disrespect routinely hurled toward me in North Carolina and occasionally toward those who supported me. It was a strenuous, distressing space to work in. The abuse of power and corruption I experienced in the District the year before weighed on me, causing me to morph from an open, friendly person into a person who was hesitant to trust people who appeared to harbor ill will or showed intrusive tendencies. I overanalyzed everything. My instincts, keenly edged, prodded me to be leery of everything and everyone. The contemptible experiences I endured in my previous school district, of which many of the cliquish parents became aware because of the research of the disgruntled parent who beset upon me as soon as I arrived, made me hyper-vigilant about doing an exceptional job. I became determined to use every leadership lesson I'd learned.

Parents in the clique the previous principal empowered didn't always treat me with respect or interact with me respectfully but I made an effort to treat them well. The situation, very complex, intensified because of parental power plays and assumptive antics that it would be business as usual as it had been with the previous principal. They remained staunchly invested in the tradition that previously guaranteed the special privileges to which they felt so entitled. I spent far too much time explaining myself and my decisions to a small group committed to misunderstanding and misinterpreting me. They nitpicked most before the school year began about classroom assignments and other special considerations. Their rationalizations covered a wide spectrum of excuses and whining. Some wanted their child or children assigned to specific teachers because an older child had been instructed by these teachers. When I countered with the explanation that all children have different learning styles, I received blank stares. Many of these parents behaved passive-aggressively when they heard the word no. They behaved politely and acceptingly while in my office only to email my supervisor or the superintendent as soon as they reached their cars or homes in furtive attempts to force my hand. Other parents used the reason that they'd "heard such great things" about the desired teacher. Usually, what they'd "heard" was sly subterfuge to conceal personal friendships with the desired teachers so their placement requests would be honored. Other than by reviewing and analyzing performance evaluations, which I did, I had no way of knowing which teachers were excellent and who needed to further develop their skill set. Truth be told, no matter how excellent a person's performance appears to be, there is always room for improvement and growth.

  What stood out to me most is that none of the parents based their requests on documented student needs or test scores. One of my most memorable conferences was with an extremely bold, overbearing mother who, with a gift in hand, cautioned me to "put my kids in the classes I'm asking for so you won't get on my bad side." I smiled, said the matter was settled and sent her on her way with her gift in hand and the same classroom assignments. Her veiled semantic threat did not frighten me. Instead, it further strengthened my resolve to break the strongholds of favoritism and privilege that were so commonplace among the favored circle of parents.

There are several reasons teacher assignment requests shouldn't be honored without extenuating circumstances. First, it's inequitable for one coterie of parents to receive special treatment while other parents have to take random assignments without question. Giving preferential treatment by honoring capricious parent requests often creates a second dilemma, cliques among teachers. As it had done at Winget Park, teacher requests empower some teachers while creating division among the others. All teachers should feel important and essential to the daily responsibilities of learning and teaching. Most importantly, as the new principal in the building, I couldn't come aboard and automatically assume teachers were doing a phenomenal job based on the number of parent requests they received. It's difficult to maintain a united front in a divided school. Many of the requests caused a rift on several grade levels because some of the teachers realized their colleagues were behind the requests. A lesson I learned previous to my appointment in Charlotte shined through this tenuous experience. An effective leader cannot compromise the trust and impartiality needed to maintain a healthy school community.

Another Southern belle behaved more insidiously than the gift-bearing mother. This mother's child experienced a potentially perilous health challenge the year before when she was left unattended. According to the student's file, the child would have died had she not been found. This parent had an unimpeachably valid reason to be angry about the incident. However, this parent's inability to move forward compounded by her stubborn refusal to trust again hindered the school's ability to work cooperatively. She felt a sense of entitlement to hold constant marathon meetings for which she wanted to command my presence as well as a high presence of faculty and staff members. In a large school with a student population over 1200 students, it's impossible for a principal to prioritize daily instruction while simultaneously attending continuous meetings for one particular student. A successful leader shares authority by delegating to and empowering members of his or her team so everyone can serve and grow. Being new to the school and all of its political dynamics, I was reluctant to set a precedent of jumping through this parent's hoops. Doing so would've created more Mayberryesque political quagmires when the next like-minded parent stepped up to the plate.

  Another memorable parent conference was with a couple up in arms when they "heard" reports about shell casings being found on school grounds one Monday morning. I'd learned quickly how alternative facts often spread quickly through our school communities. Since the school is located in a rustic area among hunters and families with guns, I didn't assume there was a plot to bring harm to the school so I waited until the police department completed its investigation to provide facts. When I didn't pander to this father as he expected me to, he became insulting.

When he asked why I wasn't upset about this "outrageous incident," I explained we were working with the police department to assess the situation and that there was no reason to panic groundlessly. The tenor of the conversation changed when he offensively quipped that perhaps I was "accustomed to violence where I came from." His wife, clearly accustomed to her husband's volatile behavior, sat silently as the rest of the incident unfolded. When I told him his comment offended me and was uncalled for and suggested that he take a breath and calm down, he began pointing his finger in my face. He became utterly discomposed, berating me, even using the low-bred phrase "you people."When I told him to remove his finger from my face, he said he would point at me all he wanted to. When this declaration failed to temper his angry antics, I decided to play his game. Feeling threatened, I walked over to the telephone, pretended to call the police and stated that I felt intense fear because an angry, menacing man was acting out violently in my face. As suddenly as it began, the parent's performance stopped and, with a face that looked as bright as volcanic lava, he told his wife they were leaving. I refused to be threatened or badgered by a rude, obstinate bully.

By no means am I belittling the importance of meeting with and working collaboratively with parents because it takes a village to educate and prepare our children. While it was refreshing to have a high level of parental involvement, far too many of the issues raised catered to petty adult issues rather than to learning and teaching, increasing teacher capacity and equitable resources for *all* students. It's reflective of what's going on throughout the nation. Adversarial behavior among many parents strikes a nerve because the needs of our children have gotten lost in the sociopolitical aspects of American educational reform.

The predominant values and beliefs at Winget Park about a principal's role baffled me. While I focused on increasing academic achievement and closing the achievement gap, too many parents harped on superficial issues like why I wasn't standing outside opening and closing car doors while waving like a political candidate and awaiting babies to kiss for staged photo opportunities. I was unwilling to be a lawn jockey who smiled, waved and opened and closed car doors when time spent meeting with parents, faculty, staff and community partners would be more professionally meaningful and critical to my purpose. Too many parents and even some faculty members became overly invested in the speed of carpool lines, appearances at Chik-Fil-A, Cold Stone Creamery and other eateries than they were in academic preparation and performance and teaching our students to use higher order thinking skills.

Some of the parents and faculty/staff waged guerilla warfare against my decision not to allow the students to wear pajamas to school the day before winter break. The tradition was wearing pajamas while watching Polar Express while eating cookies and drinking cider and hot chocolate throughout the day. I recognized the vast amount of untapped potential among the students and faculty/staff and I wanted more quality instructional time that would increase academic achievement to match up to the desired outcome of increased learning measureable in higher test scores. Teaching and learning was far more crucial before a two-week vacation than watching the same movie throughout the instructional day three years in a row. As a result, I honored the tradition but limited the film and snacks to the final ninety minutes of the day. You would think I'd put a murder for hire contract on Little Red Riding Hood on behalf of the Big Bad Wolf when I made the administrative decision to amend the tradition.

Dealing with persistent pettiness and scheming took a toll on my spirit, especially since events from the previous year still weighed heavily on my mind, so I drove either to Maryland or Virginia each weekend. I needed this time away from Charlotte to decompress. I spent time with family and friends, immersing myself in more positive, progressive environments. I listened to inspirational audio-books and chatted with friends while driving. Weekends away fortified my strength for the guaranteed challenges hurled at me during the work week. During the return drive, I prayed and focused on positive ways to combat the upcoming antics and to concentrate on what the students, faculty and staff needed.

April 2009 provided a professional crossroads. When I relocated to Charlotte, I'd planned to complete three to five years as my school's principal before exploring opportunities for growth in the school system's central office. However, the events that unfolded during a week in April broke the proverbial camel's back. During my weekly Sunday drive from Maryland to North Carolina, my mother told me my father had been diagnosed with prostate cancer. Daddy had an appointment the next day with his oncologist to determine treatment options. Those who know me are aware my father has always been my super hero. I held back tears while talking with my mother but once our call ended, the floodgates opened and became a tsunami destroying the levee holding back my emotions. I pulled off of the highway and sobbed unrestrainedly at a gas station. Once I was calm enough, I began the long green mile back to Charlotte.

The week became a blur until Thursday when I jolted by another defining moment. On Thursday afternoon, April 23, 2009, a sensationalistic news reporter arrived with news cameras in tow to address a number of half truths *about me* and our school. The reporter never made an effort prior to showing up on school grounds to interview me. Instead, he presented a one-sided, poorly researched story designed to malign my reputation as blatantly as a burning cross punctuates darkness. It was all the pitiable product of an unsubstantiated verbal lynch mob this reporter empowered on film. Remember the parent who resented me because I wouldn't kowtow to the excessive meetings for her child? Like a coward, she was the consummate cell phone gangster and she manipulated a keyboard to discredit me. Unashamed, she gleefully owned the lies she told off camera when she cackled with glee to members of the main office staff.

  The ruse of a news story was a deliberate effort to paint my reputation in a false light with the most patently absurd untruths. One accusation, which I worked in my previous school district on Mondays and Fridays and in Charlotte Tuesday through Thursday, was an incontrovertibly ignorant lie. The fact a reporter believed and reported it as truth without fact-checking defies logic and common sense. The next allegation suggested that I commuted daily from Maryland to North Carolina. No one with a third grader's working concept of geography would believe something so absurd. The third complaint, that every child and parent did not personally know me, was also preposterous. How *could* over 1200 students and their parents know me personally in eight brief months?

Despite being embarrassed *by* their ignorance and being blatantly defamed so viciously, I was also embarrassed *for* them. I persevered despite the high-tech lynching they attempted to carry out against me. When I left work the day of the newscast, I noticed one of the teachers lurking outside of the door with her stroller. This teacher, believing I would crumble, actually came back to the building to gawk at me just as people did at decaying corpses hanging after lynchings in the Old South. Looking at her hulking figure and smirking milky face, I confirmed my instincts she was one of the faculty ringleaders who so desperately wanted to bring about my demise.

The grumbling undercurrent, so obsessed with my personal business, exerted every effort to meddle in my affairs. One of the parents, a police officer's busybody wife, had her husband investigate my license plates and registration. Groundlessly running license plates is against Charlotte Mecklenburg Police departmental policy unless it involves a moving violation or suspicion of crime while driving. Once they discovered my car was registered to my parents' house, they demanded my local Charlotte address, which I refused to disclose based on my right to privacy. Because I still had a mortgage to pay in Maryland, I lived with a roommate in

North Carolina. Natalie, one of my closest friends lived in the area so I roomed with her. After the "news" story aired, Natalie reached out to the reporter to correct some of his statements. After verifying I lived in the area, the reporter asked her to share her address with him, which she refused. She also told the reporter she knew I was in town every day and that his story was utterly ridiculous and obtuse. Yet, since the reporter aired the nonfactual story without fact checking, the damage had been done. Never once did he provide a retraction to his pallet of half truths.

A group of parents supported me throughout the year despite the news broadcast and I've always been grateful. One father told the newscaster I'd probably angered the wrong housewife in The Palisades, one of the ritzier communities assigned to Winget Park. Many other parents also contacted my supervisor Dr. Cooper, the superintendent Dr. Gorman and me with emails of support. I'll never forget the Broshears family. They presented me with a prayer book and a note that said to look at these experiences as the sandpaper God was using to make me an even better person. The kindness of some supported me so greatly in light of the meanness and darkness among those who sought to bring me down.

I held my head high, remained above the fray and finished the academic year with grace. At the time it mattered most, I remained committed to being the kind of principal I chose to be rather than robotically succumbing to the desires of a small malcontented minority of parents and faculty-staff members. When I left the school, test scores had increased. We expanded as a professional learning community and we maintained a solid instructional program without teaching to the test.

The Board of Education hired and appointed me to serve as the school's instructional leader, not as a glorified party planner or diva politician who prioritized waving at cars and prancing about like a peacock over improving learning and teaching outcomes. Realizing my priorities differed drastically from those of the parents who bamboozled the reporter and those politically well-heeled enough to have Dr. Gorman's ear, I decided the day of that fateful newscast that I would resign on my terms rather than choosing to remain in a school where my experience, academic accomplishments, expertise and goals were not embraced. Combining these factors with the reality that my father had cancer and the fact I still owned a home in Maryland, I wrote my letter of resignation in May and submitted it on July 20, 2009, a month after my contract had been renewed. The politically motivated superintendent appeared more driven by a preoccupation with his image in the media rather than what was equitable and best for the children at each school. He accepted my resignation without meeting with me before I separated from the school system and without asking any background questions about what prompted the news story. Little did I know that with Gorman, the matter didn't end with my resignation letter. His acceptance wasn't an acceptance.

CHAPTER EIGHT:
It Depends On Who You Ask

"Sometimes it's surprising to find out who's trying to put the invisibility cloak on you."

Jay Z

I began applying for administrative appointments as soon as I decided to leave my position in North Carolina in May 2009. Despite applying for hundreds and hundreds of positions and successfully completing numerous interviews through my own efforts while also working with a well-known recruiter who received favorable feedback from prospective employers, I still hadn't been appointed to a position. It mystified me because I knew exactly which former supervisors I used as references. I was highly qualified, experienced and had a credible track record for increasing test scores without the taint of the cheating accusations in the District of Columbia, Atlanta and other school systems across the nation. Yet, despite interviewing well in numerous school districts and being selected as the first choice for dozens of school teams, I remained unable to move on with my professional life.

There's No Place Like Home

Naturally, I reapplied to Prince George's County Public Schools where I'd worked previously. When I was unable to return to the school system after reapplying for three years, I believed something other than the ordinary process of job applications and interviews was in play. I'd passed the Principal's Assessment several times and earned high scores.

Each of my interviews went well and the interviewing panels reassured me I would be an asset to the system. Thus, I consulted with several attorneys and entered into federal litigation against the school system. As time passes, it becomes increasingly difficult to prove human resources cases.

I didn't win the lawsuit and it became a bitter disappointment. Even the judge's ruling in the case appeared prejudicial. He dismissed the case by ruling that I don't look patently Latina. This statement is biased on its face. All Latino people don't look any more alike than all Black or White people do. There are Hispanic people who resemble white people and Afro Latino people who look like the colorful spectrum of Black American people.

Winning the War of Information Can Be A Bigger Victory

Although I didn't win the lawsuit, I discovered a treasure trove of evidence that proved I'd been blackballed; thus, illegally prevented from acquiring gainful employment. Some battles are worth fighting even when you lose. In that respect, while I lost the court battle, I won the war of information. Initially, the loss depressed me because I'd invested my heart, time and hope first in applying for employment and in winning the case. My counsel allowed me to work closely with them while preparing the case and the knowledge I gained is invaluable. One of the most vital lessons I learned is the value of depositions and the wealth of knowledge they provide. Think of a deposition as an opportunity to ask questions and tap into all of the information the other side is trying to hide. During depositions, testimony is taken from fact witnesses who are under oath as if they would be while testifying in a court of law before a judge. Depositions reveal the details opposing counsel seeks to manipulate to their advantage. They're puzzle pieces of truth and every piece matters.

Let's Play Ball

The school system's counsel presented an entertaining cast of characters and documents to defend their position. My legal team quickly recognized multiple pretextual arguments opposing counsel presented. Pretextual arguments, the reasons presented to defend what the person or organization being sued has used to justify what it has done, are always fertile soil to till. The second vital lesson I learned is how essential it is to pick pretexts apart. The Thatcher Firm, at that time counsel for the school system, presented a litany of reasons in defense of the school system's actions. Each pretext pointed to a common denominator as the facts emerged during depositions as to why and how key central office figures collaborated to prevent rehiring me as an administrator.

Pretext Upon Pretext

The first pretext was a letter allegedly written by Dr. William R. Hite, the school system's most recently departed superintendent. In this mysterious letter, dated December 3, 2008, Dr. Hite claimed I was ineligible for hire because I'd resigned my position "in lieu of termination." I resigned in 2005 when I accepted a principalship in the District of Columbia Public Schools based on my performance and our school's accomplishments in Prince George's County Public Schools. This phantom letter would have been a viable argument eloquently wrapped with a bow *had it been true*. Several of Dr. Hite's statements negate the alleged letter's validity. First, he stated, "Ms. Barbour, it is my understanding that your resignation was prompted as a compromise to a pending unsatisfactory performance evaluation. This has been validated and documented in coordination and conversation with your former Regional Area Superintendent."

His statements are misleading and patently false. When I resigned, I submitted my letter of resignation directly to the Chief of Human Resources. This was proper protocol because only authorized human resources personnel can officially hire and fire personnel and officially accept letters of resignation while all other personnel only make recommendations. I did not have a conversation with my supervisor at the time I separated from the school system because she was on vacation. Second, according to school system policy and procedure and the collective bargaining agreement with the administrators union, when an employee officially resigns in lieu of termination, it happens only after an official Laudermill hearing among the employee, the school system's labor relations designee and the employee's union and/or legal representation. I never attended a hearing because I had not committed a terminable offense for which there was a need to resign. Thus, this pretext was false and negates the validity of Hite's phantom letter.

Many organizations prepare phantom letters to cover their tracks when a lawsuit is filed. Interestingly, I never received a copy of this letter until the discovery process began in 2013. Second, how convenient Hite, a superintendent with whom I never worked, prepared a letter attacking my performance when he'd never observed it. Third and perhaps most questionable, Hite failed to name the supervisor he alleges he spoke to about me. There are only three persons he could have spoken to about me. My final supervisor, to whom I've spoken, did not speak with him about me. My other two former supervisors were in prison at the time his phantom letter "appeared" so it is highly unlikely either of them provided references.

On October 1, 2011, Shilling established a second pretext for not hiring me in her official response to the Equal Employment Opportunity Commission (EEOC). On record, she told the EEOC, "The Complainant participated in and was successful on the Principal Leadership Exercise held on July 28, 2011. The Complainant remains eligible to be called for an interview as the process for principal selection is open all year long." Most intriguingly, the official response did not include Dr. Hite's phantom letter with its documentation, the school system's first pretext.

Depositions shined a light on much more than Hite's alleged letter. My counsel selected fact witnesses to depose. Fact witnesses are those who have direct, personal knowledge about the case to which they can testify. The school system chose Synthia Shilling, Douglas Anthony and Allan Duane Arborgast. Mr. Anthony and Mr. Arborgast still worked for the school system at the time.

The Shilling Deposition

After Hite, the next character to enter the school system's little drama was Synthia Shilling, the most recent former Chief Human Resources Officer and one of the system's most colorful characters. Dr. Hite apparently had such great faith in Schilling, he appointed her to move from her position as Deputy General Counsel to become the Chief Human Resources Officer in March 2010, despite the fact she was cited in 2008 for driving while intoxicated and assaulting a state trooper by kicking him in the mouth during the traffic stop. In 2012, Shilling was convicted of failure to provide insurance information during a second driving incident for which she received one year of unsupervised probation. Everyone deserves second chances. What I find difficult to understand is how I wasn't able to get a second chance at employment with this school system as this convicted criminal who assaulted a state trooper had done with a promotion to boot.

Once appointed to the Chief's position, Dr. Hite directed Shilling to revamp the principal selection process. During her deposition, she described the process she inherited as a couple of levels of interviews with central office employees. Each candidate who completed these interviews successfully completed interviews with the school community team. The community team expressed its preferences and the superintendent would make the final decision. Shilling testified that Hite directed her to make several pivotal changes to this process. The most comprehensive change Hite directed her to make was to remove the community interview process, thereby preventing the community from weighing in on who they wanted to serve as their school's principal. Next, they added a principal assessment exercise for candidates to complete prior to their interview panel. The second layer Hite directed Shilling to implement is an interview panel format of his choosing to select principals. Only select candidates moved forward for interviews. The final step, an interview with the superintendent, became the sole deciding factor on who would have the opportunity to lead each public school. When my counsel verified on the record that school communities no longer had a voice in the decision making process, former Chief Human Resources Officer Shilling testified without hesitation that this change wasn't her idea. This is pivotal moving forward because Hite dramatically increased his scope of power by craftily using Shilling to silence the community's voice.

When deposed on January 23, 2013, Shilling appeared confused at times. At times, she acted unsure whether I was a school system employee at the time of the lawsuit. Clearly, opposing counsel prepared her before she gave her deposition so it became obvious she couldn't recall details accurately. The deposition soon became quite adversarial. The purpose of a deposition is to clarify information. Yet when my counsel asked questions about the EEOC Response Shilling prepared in her official capacity, opposing counsel Robert Baror became obstinately determined to prevent my attorneys from getting answers. After spouting objections through an infuriated crimson face, opposing counsel growled, "I am instructing her not to answer anything about the intent or meaning of this document. It speaks for itself. It was prepared by her in her attorney capacity. She is not being deposed as an attorney, what her advocacy meant or was intended to convey." When my attorney sought clarification on what role she was being deposed, opposing counsel continued to equivocate, snapping, "You called her. She is a fact witness according to you." He behaved like a huffy toddler in the midst of an epic temper tantrum, all the while impetuously disrupting the former Chief's testimony. I believe he was determined to conceal points of fact Shilling, the only person who had explicit knowledge about the Response she prepared, could provide. Opposing counsel cunningly claimed Shilling prepared the Response as an attorney in order to prevent her from providing accurate testimony, using client privilege to cloak the truth. She happened to *be* an attorney but she was not functioning *as an attorney* at the time she prepared and submitted the official EEOC Response.

    My frustration with opposing counsel's interpretation of the points of fact intensified during this portion of the deposition. At the beginning of her deposition, the former Chief testified that the Chief's position was her final job prior to resigning. When asked about her duties, she stated, "everything related to Human Resources. So I managed three departments, Human Resources Operations, Human Capital Management and Employee Labor Relations. So everything from hiring people to evaluating people, to firing people." Yet, despite stating such specific criteria about her duties, she later tried to reinterpret them once the EEO Response became Exhibit One. Once my counsel asked probative questions, the answers that provide the meat one side wants to discover that the other wants to conceal, Shilling supported opposing counsel's campaign to block us from getting the truth by saying she had served as the Chief but still also performed all of the duties she had as Deputy General Counsel.

This sounded like a flat lie. In earlier testimony she testified she was Deputy General Counsel *until* she moved into the Chief's position, which sounds like a clear transition of duties. Either she testified truthfully when she said her final position was Chief Human Resources Officer from March 2010 until August 2012, or she lied when subsequently testifying she worked as the Chief *and* performed all of the duties of Deputy General Counsel. According to Board of Education policy and procedure, an employee cannot serve in more than one official capacity at a time. In my opinion based on Shilling's testimony, I believe opposing counsel suborned perjury by setting forth a distraction of combined duties to invoke attorney-client privilege and using the work product doctrine as a crutch to prevent Shilling from providing full, accurate testimony.

Legal privilege, which opposing counsel doggedly invoked, protects communication between a client and an attorney, although privilege belongs to the client rather than the lawyer. The work product privilege, a legal concept that prevents opposing counsel from compelling discovery about written materials an attorney prepared, is how the Baror manipulated testimony about the EEO Response. This crafty legal maneuver magnified a serious conflict of interest. Schilling as the deponent used an unclear transition of duties as a way to avoid testifying and thereby became incapable of serving as a fact witness. Further, if she was not truly functioning as the Chief Human Resources Officer, then the EEO Response was nullified. However, when an attorney is not acting as direct legal counsel, privilege doesn't apply. Such is the case with this deponent. The fact that Shilling has a law degree is irrelevant to her capacity since the position of Chief Human Resources Officer did not require legal expertise.

The Anthony Deposition

On February 26, 2013, we deposed Douglas Anthony, the acting Chief Human Resources Officer. Anthony replaced Shilling upon her departure from Prince George's County Public Schools. He was much more willing and able to clearly articulate Human Resources policies and procedures than his predecessor. As did his predecessor, Anthony spoke quite often about Dr. Hite and his omnipresent role in principal selection and hiring. He testified repeatedly about how Hite had the ultimate and final say about principal selection. First, Anthony testified, "So the superintendent will make the final selection and is not required to select an individual from the recommended candidates is always the case. So, to be honest, we can have this whole process and the superintendent can go into a school and say, I want this teacher to be a principal at this school. So it always supersedes any process we have in place."

This is a powerfully telling statement. The consistent theme between the two depositions thus far was the level absolute power and control Hite seized and wielded. The most significant statement our second material witness made was in response to my counsel's question about whether the superintendent's phantom letter prevented me from employment with the school system. He responded, "I'll answer it this way. It hasn't prevented us from considering her application or letting her apply for the position." It became abundantly clear as each succeeding piece of the puzzle emerged that Hite played an intentional role in preventing me from returning to the school system. The question quickly became why.

The Arborgast Deposition

With a calculated move, opposing counsel stalled the third deposition until the final day of discovery. Discovery, the time where both sides obtain evidence about the other party, is the endgame for all depositions. On March 13, 2013, Allan Duane Arborgast, the final deponent testified. Once again Hite became the common denominator of testimony. As the Chief Academic Officer during the time I applied for rehire, Dr. Arborgast testified, "The superintendent and I probably met weekly about personnel and about people moving into other positions. And then at this point, in conversation with the superintendent, this was a candidate we decided not to pursue." When my counsel asked the witness to elaborate on his discussion with the superintendent, he responded, "So, I don't remember the exact details and I don't remember why we decided not to pursue her. I don't remember that level of detail. But I remember that this was a person we were not going to pursue." When asked if the superintendent knew who I was, he replied, "Yes, he had some knowledge of her."

My counsel pressed further, asking about the phantom letter. Opposing counsel became short-tempered once again, defensively interjecting, "And I'll be happy to represent that there is nobody who works for the school system who has any knowledge beyond the four corners of this document." Opposing counsel became quite defensive once again about this document, one he provided on behalf of his client. When my counsel asked the Arborgast if the letter prevented me from becoming a principal, his answer somewhat mirrored Anthony's. He said, "Well, it's my understanding that Ms. Barbour applied for these positions and took the principal exercises. So this letter certainly didn't stop that process."

When my counsel reminded Arborgast of his earlier testimony that the superintendent had the final say in hiring principals, he added to his earlier testimony, "Absolutely. We wouldn't argue. Even if I did disagree, I wouldn't argue with him." His next statement is not only disturbing but it also appears to represent how a systemic practice based on Board of Education policy and procedure had been overstepped at will. He verified on record that, "Human Resources is supposed to check the references and make sure the reference letters are there." Next, he launched a seemingly eternal harangue that shed a quite disconcerting spotlight on the Prince George's County School system's human resources practices. Arborgast testified that it's his "personal experience is reference letters are not particularly discriminating." He explained his opinion about what makes a reference letter "discriminating." He continued, "So what I do is I look for who wrote the letter. And then, do I have a respect for that person? I either have respect for them or don't have respect for them or don't know them. So you're looking for that kind of relationship." His testimony didn't end there. "But there are certainly individuals that if I received a reference letter or call from that person, I'd give that serious weight."

When my counsel asked if any other forms of reference are considered, the witness eagerly answered, "Oh yeah. So there would be calls. There's an informal network around references. And as you work in this business, you develop this informal network around references. And as you work in this business, you develop this network for references. And to keep your integrity, you want to make sure that when you're in the network, you're brutally honest. You can do that on a phone, wherein you wouldn't necessarily do that in a letter. I also sometimes call people who are not listed as references if I have a relationship in that district." Arborgast, along with Hite, was a part of the Broad Group network, the alternative superintendent preparation program we discussed earlier.

Arborgast provided a transcript of an abundance of human resources violations. It utterly shocked me an executive level employee would incriminate himself and other executive level employees as to how they willfully violated policies, procedures and best practices. Only references listed by an applicant should be legally contacted. Second, Prince George's County Public School's Board of Education policies and procedures specifically stipulate that Human Resources specialists are the only personnel designated to speak with and verify references. The coincidence that an executive level employee is friends with or in a network with someone who "knows" an applicant does not make sidebar conversations acceptable in a professional setting. This "network" connection also doesn't mean their reference is superior to or more informed than those provided by applicants from references who actually worked directly with an applicant.

Arborgast's next statement let the proverbial cat out of the bag. When my counsel asked if anyone at the executive level contacted an unlisted reference, he made no effort to deny it. "I am aware our superintendent and the superintendent from her last district had a conversation." Peter Gorman, my former superintendent from Charlotte Mecklenburg Public Schools, also a Broad superintendent was a part of Hite and Arborgast's networks. He named the superintendent, adding, "I think it was a negative reference." Not one to value brevity as the mark of genius, Arborgast shared precise comments about Hite's thought processes on negative references. When asked to validate how he knew what Hite thought, strangely there was no objection from opposing counsel. He elaborated for the record, "Because I've seen it. So I've seen – so he would have formed an opinion on individuals and we wouldn't move on that. He was – had a lot of connections. He has a pretty vast network." The network the witness referred to includes the superintendent's connections with The Broad Academy as well as with New Leaders for New Schools and Teach for America.

  Things became most interesting during the final portion of this deposition following the witness' lunch break with Robert Baror and the EEO Compliance Officer Elizabeth Davis. Curiously, Arborgast became very strategic and succinct in his responses. He tried to take back the puzzle pieces so eagerly laid on the table during earlier testimony. It was startling to watch him revert from his earlier verbosity while describing Hite's intricate network, unyielding opinions and alleged conversation with Peter Gorman. When my counsel probed for further details about his alleged conversation with the superintendent, Arborgast testified, "I don't remember his exact words and I'm not actually sure he said it to me or to one of the other chiefs." His reversal, so well-timed for opposing counsel, baffled my attorney and me. The more questions my counsel asked, the more obvious and impenetrable Arborgast's backtracking became. His reversal became more steadfast when he shared under oath, "What I'm saying is, it became known but I don't recall an active conversation with the superintendent. I just remember in our conversation between the Chief Human Resources Officer, the superintendent and me, it was decided not to – it was communicated to me that we're not going to consider it." When asked who communicated to him I wouldn't be hired, Arborgast stuck to his new testimony like a tick to a dog's back. He insisted he didn't know and couldn't remember who said what or whether the comments had been directed to him.

  My attorney immediately noticed the shift during this portion of Arborgast's testimony so she refreshed his memory with the record of his earlier testimony. As opposing counsel attempted to object, he testified, "I actually don't recall having a conversation with the superintendent about Ms. Barbour." When asked again, he responded, "I don't recall. I actually had not remembered Ms. Barbour's name until this came up. I had completely – I hadn't given it a lot of thought. So when we started going through the depositions, you know, where is this. And we had said we weren't going to consider her. And that would've come from the superintendent or the Chief Human Resources Officer. But I actually don't recall our conversation specifically about Carol Barbour."

I'd never witnessed anyone reverse themselves under oath after such detailed testimony about how efficiently networks can be used. It was much like television drama written for a stunning Law and Order SVU courtroom scene between Rafael Barba and a reluctant witness. When asked again about the negative reference he discussed earlier, Arborgast responded, "Yeah, so there was – I was aware there was a negative reference from North Carolina but I don't recall if it was the conversation I had with the superintendent or a conversation I had with the Chief. I just recall there was a negative reference from North Carolina."

My counsel sought further clarification. Arborgast next stated he became aware of the conversation between Hite and Gorman while preparing for the deposition and added, "I do remember the negative reference, and from North Carolina. And I do remember the criticism of Ms. Barbour in a Google search. But the – I don't remember how it came to my knowledge." How unusual his memory became so muddled in a matter of hours. It appeared he had been directed to provide a different testimony after lunch with opposing counsel.

The Google search to which he referred is the sensationalistic newspaper article from North Carolina that had never been properly vetted. Once again, Arborgast demonstrated how established human resources policies and practices had been broken. Educated, experienced appointees like Arborgast and Hite should know better than to rely solely on Google searches and one-sided information. How many other applicants to Prince George's County Public Schools and so many others around the country have been railroaded and blackballed by superintendents or other executive level employees and their networks? I suppose it depends who you ask.

CHAPTER NINE:
It's No Fun When the Rabbit's Has the Gun

"I like fly shit, you like gossip
I let you do you, Why you ridin' my shit?"

Jay Z,
"Jockin' Jay Z"

Duck and Dodge, Bob and Weave

After depositions, the school system's most recently former superintendent William R. Hite emerged as the common denominator. Every well-manicured finger pointed directly to Hite during each deposition. As a result of the written record, my legal team decided to depose Hite since he was the common thread holding opposing counsel's defense together. Despite multiple requests and summons to complete his deposition, he ducked and dodged each attempt. On March 23, 2013, two weeks after the bombshell deposition nullifying the phantom letter and each additional pretext offered, the superintendent opportunely submitted a sworn affidavit to opposing counsel that mirrored testimony from the final deposition. Under penalty of perjury, he made claims of an alleged telephone conversation with my former superintendent, his fellow Broad alumnus. In the affidavit, Hite said:

> I knew the Superintendent. Therefore, I gave him a call to inquire about Ms. Barbour. He provided a negative reference regarding Ms. Barbour. He specifically said that Ms. Barbour was "one of the worst principals he had ever been associated with" and he said she was "terrible." As a result of his negative reference, I instructed the Chief Human Resources Officer to remove Ms. Barbour's name from any list of candidates for positions to ensure she was not hired.

Gorman Wasn't Listed As A Reference

Hite's admissions in the affidavit are troubling for multiple reasons. First, I did not list Gorman as a reference. He never visited my school or observed me so he had no direct knowledge of my performance. Second, it appears Hite not only used an unauthorized absence but also entertained hearsay instead of looking for and determining facts. Third, opposing counsel provided this affidavit two weeks *after* the final deponent's testimony. My attorneys believed its timing was far beyond coincidental, especially given the fact that opposing counsel knew we wanted to depose Hite ourselves. Though opposing counsel can conveniently claim they had no knowledge of Hite's conversation prior to Arborgast's deposition, the claim isn't very believable because of the level of detail Arborgast used while backpedaling and reversing his testimony, almost as if to set a precedent for their pretext.

Which, If Any of Your Stories, Are True?

This opportune affidavit also calls into question the truthfulness of the school system's EEO Response when the record said, "The Complainant remains eligible to be called for an interview as the process for principal selection is open all year long." Shilling, The Chief Human Resources Officer and first deponent, prepared the Response a year *after* the superintendent testified via affidavit that he directed her to "ensure she was not hired." Why spin a different web for the EEO? It is clear Shilling followed Hite's directive to blackball me. Consequently, the opportune affidavit also questions the accuracy of Schilling's deposition when she testified, "I can't say for sure," when asked when she first became aware of my name. It's unlikely a Chief Human Resources Officer would forget being directed to blacklist an applicant unless it was a common systemic practice to capriciously blackball potential employees. Interestingly, Arborgast testified quite vividly about the conversations to blackball me, including the fact Shilling had been present at the time.

Did Any of My Letters of Reference Count?

Points of fact, superintendents like Hite work at the pleasure of school boards and as such, are required to follow and enforce school board policies and procedures. According to human resources policy and procedure in Prince George's County Schools and most other systems, only human resources specialists are authorized to verify and contact references to avoid complaints and lawsuits. Arborgast's lengthy testimony about the value of one's network and contacting friends who aren't listed as references, Hite's well-timed affidavit and the order he gave to blacklist me as a candidate makes it clear there was an attempt to circumvent the established human resources protocols that safeguard applicants and guarantee transparency and consistency throughout the process.

It is evident that neither Hite nor his executive appointees Schilling and Arborgast reviewed my written references without bias, nor did they bother to ask follow up questions. Instead, by his own words in his affidavit, Hite chose to engage in an outside personal conversation with a colleague. This is also an example of how Hite used his position to inappropriately influence the principal selection process and eliminate community input across the school system. Two of the three deponents specifically testified that the superintendent's word stood unopposed. Why adopt a hiring process if you're not going to follow it? As John Dalberg Acton said, "Power tends to corrupt, and absolute power corrupts absolutely."

Can't Make This Story Right

Had he been a fair-minded leader who valued truth and a balanced view, Hite would have followed policy and procedure, reviewed my references and asked me about my time in Charlotte. As a part of the application process, the appropriate human resources personnel had reviewed my reference letters and contacted my references prior to Hite involving himself. A thorough review of my performance and record of accomplishments and achievements would have addressed many of his concerns.

Reference Letter, Former Supervisor

For example, one of my former supervisors who regularly interacted with me wrote the following reference letter:

Carol is dependable and has high standards. Her work ethic is high. I can readily describe Carol as politically astute, analytical and highly organized. When she is given a directive she will follow it through although she can be trusted to implement systemic policies and procedures with autonomy. As the principal of a Title I elementary school with a high ESL population, high-quality teaching and learning is crucial to Carol because she knows her students must be prepared to compete in the real world. Instructional leadership is the principal's responsibility about which she is most passionate.

Establishing and maintaining community partnerships is also one of Carol's priorities. To date, she has five very active partnerships that include faith-based partnerships and corporate as well as non-profit partnerships. Carol realizes the importance of collaborating with the community to make her school a rich center of learning.

Carol has grown and matured greatly as a leader over the past three years. It was a pleasure to serve as her supervisor and mentor.

Reference Letter, Community Partner

This letter from a community partner should also have been considered.

> This letter of recommendation is prepared for Ms. Carol F. Barbour. I have known Carol for six years. When she was a principal in our school system, she worked collaboratively with the police department in order to improve conditions in the communities where her students lived. She was so dedicated to making a better community for the faculty, staff, parents and students, she received a Commander's Award for Community Leadership on June 11, 2005. At that time I was the District Commander.
>
> Seeing her passion for her students and her dedication to the community firsthand, I appointed her to the District III Commander's Citizen Advisory Task Force in 2004. During her membership on the task force, she provided input on how the community could work together to make our schools a safer, sounder place, dialogued with officials and answered questions and addressed concerns and pitched in during many of the department's seminars.

These are excerpts from two of multiple letters of reference on file at the time Hite deliberately chose to blacklist me and deny employment. Had he followed established policies and procedures as he was contractually bound to do, Hite would have relied on human resources professionals to review my references.

Gorman's Role

Let's examine the role Peter Gorman, my former superintendent in Charlotte Mecklenburg Public Schools played. When my legal team received the affidavit, we initiated legal proceedings against both men in order to drill down to the truth. For the record, I did not initially believe Dr. Gorman engaged in the alleged conversation until I reflected on the blueprint Arborgast so amply provided during his deposition. I believe *if* the affidavit reflected an actual conversation, Dr. Gorman never expected it to become fodder for a legal strategy. Board of Education policy and procedure for Charlotte Mecklenburg Public Schools also requires that references are verified through human resources. Further, according to the North Carolina human resources department database, I am classified as eligible for rehire. While writing this book, I obtained official paperwork that evidences my eligibility to return to Charlotte Mecklenburg Public Schools if I chose to do so.

I spent nine months working in Charlotte. That's hardly enough time for a superintendent to unilaterally label a former employee as "one of the worst principals he had ever been associated with" and "terrible." During the time I spent there, Dr. Gorman *never* once visited my school. He *never* personally discussed a single academic or operational concern with me. He *never* observed or evaluated my performance. He *never* offered feedback or suggestions for growth and he never identified or discussed any performance deficits.

Charlotte-Mecklenburg Resignation Letter

When I resigned my position, my supervisor recommended that I summarize the accomplishments my faculty, staff, students, community partners and I made during the academic year. This is the letter I submitted:

I am resigning my position as principal with deep regret. When I joined the school system, I never anticipated I would be unable to sell my home. Unfortunately, I can no longer sustain living expenses in both Maryland and North Carolina. My year has been both challenging and rewarding. I became unexpectedly ill in December and had to have surgery. Further exacerbating matters, I developed a life-threatening post-surgical complication that forced me to take much longer than I wanted to recuperate. My father was diagnosed with cancer, a difficult but galvanizing crisis for my family. However, despite of all of the odds, your strategic vision coupled with my supervisor's leadership and support were guiding principles for me as an instructional leader. I also benefitted greatly by working with my coach. As a result, here are just a few of <u>our</u> accomplishments in a single academic year:

- Reorganization and realignment of staffing that included special area teachers in the corrective reading program for students in tested grades,

- Implemented longer reading and mathematics instructional blocks, resulting in increased student achievement,
- Created EC/ESL inclusion classes to more efficiently use teachers, resulting in an increase in academic achievement among all subgroups and a narrowing of the achievement gap,
- Based on first-year SQR data, I designed and presented professional development to establish teacher capacity with data disaggregation, to increase academic rigor during instructional delivery and to increase rigor and differentiation in written assignments, resulting in a significant increase in student performance on end of grade tests,
- Established and enforced high expectations for faculty and staff members and began the documentation process to remove ineffective persons,
- Realigned roles for facilitators to move from serving as observers to serving as teacher leaders who coached their colleagues and monitored the integrity of the instructional program,
- Implemented Professional Learning Communities, establishing collaborative practices increase team work and build teacher capacity, resulting in teachers beginning to create common assessments as grade levels. Teachers also began making data-driven learning and teaching decisions and using Acuity as learning tool between school and the home.
- Posted the first school-wide data wall to visually remind teachers of the amount of progress each child in our school needed to make,
- Created and implemented a daily Principal's Award to motivate students and recognize their academic accomplishments and citizenship.

Accomplishments I Didn't List

There were other accomplishments too. I began and completed the documentation process to remove ineffective employees. I'll share the most colorful example. One of the teachers displayed erratic behaviors that had been documented in their personnel file. Before I became the school's principal, this teacher cursed at a parent and in a second incident, cursed at maintenance workers. The next year, the teacher admitted to snatching a marker from a child and throwing it across the table. During the year I served as principal, I received multiple student and parent complaints about alleged profanity and temper tantrums when the teacher lost control of the classroom. This teacher also allegedly called several children profane names along with at least two alleged incidents of physical abuse. There is no valid excuse it took three years for these behaviors to be dealt with. Yet, it did.

During my year in Charlotte, I worked continuously with a retired regional superintendent and with my supervisor, the current regional superintendent. Both visited the school consistently and observed my performance firsthand in areas where I excelled, needed to grow and where I met resistance from faculty, staff and community members determined to oppose change.

Leadership Coach's Input

In an excerpt of the letter of reference she wrote for me, my leadership coach stated:

> The problem Ms. Barbour faced as she became principal was student achievement was significantly lower than the ability of the students. She also faced both a staff and parent population highly invested in keeping things exactly the way they had been done before. Consistently, she made decisions based on increasing student achievement. Change was difficult. She has built support among both staff members and parents while dealing with those who continue to be disgruntled.
>
> I have been especially impressed with Ms. Barbour's understanding of teacher instruction and student learning. Dialoguing with her during an instructional walkthrough allows one to see how she understands instruction and is able to diagnose and provide recommendations for improving student learning. She uses these skills in observing teachers and helping them to grow professionally as a result of her observations and suggestions.
>
> I would recommend Ms. Barbour for an Elementary Principalship or for any educational position related to teaching and learning.

Terrible? Really?

What a difference visiting a school on a regular basis and directly observing an employee's performance makes. If increasing academic achievement, making the school a safer place by properly documenting and executing staffing changes collaboratively with human resources and setting and holding high expectations makes me "one of the worst principals he had been associated with" and "terrible," so be it. *If* Gorman made the statements Hite says he did and used to direct employees to blacklist me, they're unfounded by proven facts and based on conclusions drawn he never presented to, discussed with or gave me an opportunity to clarify.

Unfortunately, one affidavit and an unsubstantiated news article have temporarily altered the trajectory of my career. Tragically, this happens to many educational leaders across the nation who have also reaped the consequences of unfounded information. In an age of the internet and social media when people are free to spew vitriol about others virtually without consequence, circumstances are rife for damaging people's reputations, particularly among maverick politicians and superintendents who appear to be quite comfortable with playing fast and loose with school system policies and procedures and prematurely rushing to judgment about others. How many other employment candidates have been negatively painted with a broad brush?

Consider the following passage about Dr. Gorman in an online statement from which he had little to no defense.

> The newspaper has a story today on the idiot in charge of our NC Schools. His idea of improvement in these desperate economic times is to spend two million dollars of money he doesn't have for a bunch of needless, abusive and unjustifiable tests at a time when schools are struggling to hold on to teachers and even their photocopy budgets.
>
> Who is he and why should parents tell him to Go to Hell? He is another one of those corporate kool-aid drinking dip dogs trained by the Broad Toads (Class of 2004) to undermine the ethos in care in schools, to bust teacher unions and teacher professionalism and to put public schools in the hands of Theory X corporate managers with social agendas circa 1950.

These aren't flattering passages by any means. During the academic year I spent in Charlotte as one of Gorman's principals, I can attest that he's definitely not an idiot. He also wasn't a union buster since North Carolina is a right to work state.

Should we ever believe what one person says about another, either personally or on the internet, without fact checking? Absolutely not. It's never right to disparage and belittle others. Sometimes we'll never know how it feels until the rabbit has the gun and takes a shot.

CHAPTER TEN:
Fallout ... Too Many Unanswered Questions

> "I now realize that lives fall apart when they need to be rebuilt. Lives fall apart when the foundation upon which they were built needs to be relaid. Lives fall apart, not because God is punishing us for what we have or have not done. Lives fall apart because they need to. They need to because they weren't built the right way in the first place."
>
> Iyanla Vanzant,
> *Peace from Broken Pieces*

Countless questions haunted me. How had these horrible things happened to me? Everything pointed to the background of my school's closure as the point of origin for it all. The closure initiated my most basic question. How had I become involved in an inappropriate relationship when I knew better from the start? The answer, both simple and plain, emerged quickly.

We make decisions at the level of our self-esteem and happiness. After having painful, horrible experiences one after another, my self-esteem plummeted so deeply it almost evaporated. I felt such a primal need to connect with someone after experiencing the heartbreak and loneliness of my ex-husband's betrayal, the humiliation of the child he fathered with his girlfriend, our subsequent divorce and his e decision to marry her before our divorce decree dried. I worked a stressful but demanding job I loved and prioritized. I threw myself into my work. It became my life. Consequently, my need for connection and intimacy overrode my sense of right and wrong. It was inconceivable to me that I'd engaged in an inappropriate relationship with another woman's husband when I so intimately understood how deeply that pain hurts from my own experiences. Hindsight is always twenty-twenty and so very instructive. The indiscretion I engaged in, while passionate and fulfilling of my needs in the moment, ultimately caused some of the deepest disappointment, strife, pain and guilt I've experienced.

Michelle Rhee didn't have the right to capriciously close a public school in retaliation for my refusal to answer questions about my private life on behalf of Lanier. Yet, she did. Former police chief Cathy Lanier didn't have the right to divulge information from an open investigation, share hearsay about my personal life or use the Chancellor as a pawn against me. Yet, she did. The Interloper had no right to attempt to interrogate me about police matters as a civilian. Yet, she did. She also should not have been privy to who had been "fired" prior to those affected. Yet, she was. She had no right to share personnel decisions that had yet to be announced through email. Yet, she did. These are all facts.

Yet, no matter how inappropriate their actions were, I had to face the consequences and realities of my actions that did not justify but created the window of opportunity for Rhee, Lanier and The Interloper to do the things they did. Consequences always present themselves but rarely as we believe they should. My consequences brought anger and guilt. I felt paralyzed with fear and powerless to do anything to help my community fight the closure. At the time, Rhee and Lanier enjoyed second tier popularity as the mayor's untouchable favorites and local media darlings so there was no way to tangibly fight back. Their popularity created a climate where no one would believe either of these women made a mistake, let alone believe they behaved collusively to transform a personal situation into a professional matter, Lanier for personal gain and Rhee simply because Lanier asked her to.

There was also The Interloper who fancied herself a community activist while using her access to the Rhee, Lanier and countless other elected and appointed officials to exploit and punish citizens she believed had insulted or wronged her.

I'd never been silent in the face of adversity so feeling unable to act in these burdensome circumstances made me feel alone, powerless and inconsolable. Despite my fear and apprehension, I immediately began quietly fighting for my legal rights. I retained an attorney who filed an appeal on my behalf as a first step. Rohulamin Quander, one of the senior administrative judges at the Office of Employee Appeals (OEA) ruled on September 30, 2008, the allegations against Rhee and other key persons may have a legal remedy but he could not make a decision in the matter. I also filed an EEOC complaint and waited 845 days – two years and three months – for an incomplete investigation and the resulting Right to Sue letter.

I don't know what frustrated me most while I awaited completion of the EEOC investigation. The investigator showed indifference and nonchalance. The dismissive, flippant excuses presented to justify the 845 days I waited would frustrate the most patient person. The other explanation for the shoddy investigation seemed much more plausible. The school district failed to provide documentation and they did not have my personnel file when the investigator requested it. It seems the investigator didn't complete the investigation because she didn't receive the information she needed to do so.

The EEOC isn't the only organization that has had to wait for the school district to comply. The court case filed in 2009 remained open in federal court until December 2017 because the school system's counsel has continuously filed delays, motions and briefs at an enormous cost to taxpayers and to the plaintiffs. While my colleagues and I awaited legal justice, a deferred dream for nearly a decade, I've gained more of the strength needed to stand tall and share my story. As Talib once said, "We have to become anti-fragile, or die."

Even when I moved on to the position in Charlotte, an appointment for which I felt grateful, it became impossible to release the bundle of emotions I felt. I thought so much of my old school and my regrets because I'd been pushed out of a job and school community I loved. Rhee's demeaning, exaggerated words about the school district's employees had been heard and read throughout most major news outlets and multiple television shows. There virtually wasn't an urban school system to which I could apply that hadn't been privy to and/or influenced by the Rhee's words and anecdotes. Her words carried much more weight than her under-experienced opinion should have. Her appearance on The Oprah Winfrey Show elevated Rhee to new heights as a darling educator while simultaneously damning educators on whose backs she built a false educational reform. When you've been denounced by a person Oprah thinks is just great, there are damaging repercussions. Each of these stressors made it increasingly difficult to focus on my new opportunity.

It was impossible to pretend everything would be alright … because it wasn't. The pain of rejection, hopelessness and the degradation of long-term unemployment nearly destroyed me. I'd never felt like a failure and here I was, young, knowledgeable and viable in my early forties wearing a scarlet letter U for unemployed. I treaded uncharted waters unlike any I'd previously encountered. The pain and degradation of unemployment and the circumstances in which everything unfolded weighed heavily on me. I felt trapped in a never ending cycle of post traumatic stress disorder and anxiety attacks because no matter what I did and no matter how hard I tried, I just couldn't move forward.

In addition to the shambles I called a personal life, I experienced one of the deepest periods of fear, anger and bitterness I'd ever had because of the way my school had been closed. It was as if the blueprints our leadership team reviewed and envisioned coming to fruition during the renovation had never existed. It was as if the funding allotted to our school for renovation had utterly disappeared. These painful experiences along with the routine stressors of school leadership proved an enormous burden that became increasingly difficult to bear. I didn't want my time at that school to end. We'd made tangible strides as a team and we remained committed to make many more.

My unresolved pain from the previous years of struggle and oppression reared its proverbially ugly head and blended with the fresh challenges within my new environment. I faced persistent encounters with white privilege from a small but determined group of parents so heavily invested in preserving the power of authority they'd exercised with impunity. There was also dissension among a small yet vocal group of faculty and staff and their supporting parents who felt content with passing scores. They didn't recognize the need I felt to increase academic performance with instructional rigor and to set and maintain higher expectations among all student groups. They didn't respect the central office mandate for me to increase academic performance either.

Once my year in Charlotte ended turbulently, I realized it was time to reevaluate, regroup and try to return home to work. I believed I would quickly secure another administrative appointment. My hope crushed and optimism eventually shattered. For years I tried to find another job but doors slammed in my face continuously.

The feelings of worthlessness and self-loathing intermingled with the two stress-ridden years I experienced back to back. I declined from the happy, successful and vital woman who managed my stress into a bitter, depressed, lethargic shell of who I'd once been. I felt trapped beneath the weight of it all. No matter how diligently I tried, it felt nearly impossible to take two steps forward because I felt discouraged and blocked at every turn. I completed three years of successful competency examinations, every level of interviews and emerged as a top choice for many school communities in the DMV. Yet, I had nothing to show for it. Never had I experienced such a bottomless pit of hopelessness. In my mind, I'd become an abysmal failure. I felt useless, dejected, abandoned and forsaken, even by God.

On a humid summer day in 2017, I realized the pain had to end. Tired and worn down, the black pit of rejection enveloped me, becoming a current of sadness I could no longer swim against. Every moment of pain guilt and sadness I'd repressed for so many years held me in bondage. The secret I'd held onto and the shame that haunted me every day suppressed and extinguished my final glimmer of hope. I decided to give up. I didn't want to live in daily dread and disbelief another moment. Holding a bottle of Percocet in my hand, I decided to take all thirty of them that night and fall into a permanent sleep. I spent the morning cleaning and preparing my home for my parents, family and friends when they arrived to plan my funeral and fellowship together. Throughout the afternoon and early evening, I wrote personal letters to my mother and father and to those closest to me. I wanted to say goodbye and remind everyone how much I loved them.

    Our society has such a cruel backlash toward suicide. Some of us, including me in the past, call people who express suicidal thoughts and ideations weak and selfish. Others have experienced deep trauma and are sympathetic or compassionate. No matter how we feel about suicide, it's a serious dilemma. I'm a witness we cannot continue to ignore or ridicule mental health challenges. They're as real and oppressive as any physical health challenge.

    That evening, I got into bed, took the cap off of my pill bottle and poured the pills on my nightstand. I picked up my water bottle, unscrewed the top and took a sip of water. Just as I was about to take the first handful of pills, the phone rang. My mentor Doris Reed called to chat. Ms. Reed suggested I expand my job search so I could cast my skills and experience with a wider net. We had such a long chat while sharing joyful laughter, I fell asleep on the phone. When I woke up the next morning, I decided to spend my final day alone and carry out my plan that evening.

    What I intended to be my last day was a gorgeous day. The sky, boldly blue, became a tapestry for the fluffy cotton candy-like clouds. Perhaps my intent to end my life that night prompted me to notice the beauty around me for the first time in what felt like eons. Lunch with wine at the Cheesecake Factory became my last meal of choice. I enjoyed a movie and sent an Edible Arrangement to my parents.

    Later that evening, I slipped into a new pair of pajamas and climbed into bed. When I reached for my pill bottle, the phone rang. It was my parents. Out of sheer determination not to stray from the plan, I ignored the call because I knew I wouldn't have the courage to swallow those pills if I spoke to either of them. My father could always tell when something was wrong as soon as he heard my voice. Drained to the core, I wanted the pain to stop. The shame of my mistakes coupled with my inability to get a job consumed me. Considering the immense amount of time I'd dedicated to earning my education and building experience, I couldn't accept that while I ached for a second opportunity, no one would grant me one.

    Tears began falling gently down my face. I'm surprised I had any tears left since I'd cried five oceans worth already. During my evening prayers I asked God to give me a sign if He still had something valuable for me to do. It seems so naïve and misguided now to ask God for a sign not to do something He has already expressly forbidden. Yet, when rock bottom viciously confronts you, you're not thinking clearly because you're too attuned to your pain, rejection and loss. In that state of mind, it becomes increasingly difficult to hold back the bitterness and aches as they emerge from the stings of lost hope.

My phone rang again, sharply punctuating my thoughts. This time it was one of my closest girlfriends. I begrudgingly answered, determined to end the call as quickly as I could. This became quite a chore because my dear friend Renita was as chatty and bubbly as ever. During a marathon chat we laughed about college and graduate school memories, reflecting on how much we'd grown over the years. The conversation both comforted and saddened me. Once again I fell asleep without saying goodbye to the world.

Soon after I woke up the next day, my father called. This was a rare treat because he wasn't the one to spend much time on the phone. He told me he'd been unable to sleep the night before because of an intense concern about me. I broke down. I told him I'd lost my will to live, that I no longer believed I had a hopeful future. When he asked how I could be so certain my life had become hopeless, I told him I felt useless, that my faith in myself and everyone else had long dried up. I even asked him why God didn't love me anymore.

Daddy took a deep breath and reassured me I would recover all I'd lost if I changed my *mindset* and *focus*. He reminded me how vital it is to remain hopeful and grateful in every circumstance. He urged me to stop allowing my negative thoughts to overshadow me, to begin choosing more grateful, optimistic thoughts. I'd pretended to be alright and held so tightly to that façade for so long without realizing that virtually anyone who interacted with me could sense my brokenness and vulnerability. Self-pity, long term unemployment, inactivity and years of rejection had become my badge of dishonor. What should've been a temporary detour had become a permanent roadblock.

During the months after this enlightening conversation with Daddy, I began therapy. By confronting the inner turmoil I'd been struggling to conceal, I felt the black cloud of depression that had been hanging over my life gradually began to roll away. During therapy and the time I spent healing, I had a life-propelling epiphany. In order to get on track to live the purpose God assigned me, I had to hit rock bottom. You see, hitting rock bottom reminded me I can and will live a vibrant life despite my past and my mistakes and in spite of my imperfections. Rock bottom is an inspirational time. It provides a foundation on which to refocus, rebuild and pursue the same purpose through fresh opportunities.

My time at rock bottom and reconstruction afterward reminds me that the people who retaliated against me, conspired to bring about my demise and misused me don't control me or my destiny. If anything, they did me a favor because their actions have pushed me more deeply into self-awareness, expanded my purpose and reinvigorated my faith in God. I will always be an educator. Nothing will change that. However, I'm now better equipped to lead others from rock bottom to the comebacks of their lifetimes.

Once I realized that my life would never be the same, that I would only grow and improve, I knew that my growth and development had purpose. That's when I decided to share my experiences. I had to share my story so I could rid myself of the emptiness I felt. I want to encourage the many others who've also experienced protracted difficulties and the accompanying depression and sadness so they could believe there is victory after a prolonged battle. The first word I wrote freed me from the chains of fear, rage, sadness and suicidal thoughts and ideations. The pain and damage I experienced took such a heavy toll on me that it's taken ten years to release this story publicly. Knowing the real story behind why the school permanently closed and how many other educators have been abused and mistreated in the name of educational reform, I believe it's my responsibility to share my testimony.

During my years of unemployment, I had an abundance of time to reflect on what happened and accept accountability for my actions. In the process while accepting responsibility for my actions, I realized God had forgiven me the first time I asked Him to. It was then I became able to forgive those who wronged me and, also importantly, to forgive myself.

Our fortitude as a group became a reality when we won a financial settlement against the Government of the District of Columbia in late 2017. Nearly a decade later, victory came through the court system, yet some of us still suffer the effects of the court of public opinion. As soon as I became free of the legal obligation to wait, I decided to tell my story. If I can save another teacher, principal or child from being harmed by the very institutions meant to empower us to greatness, my experience will not have been in vain.

PART THREE:
I'M NOT THE ONLY EDUCATOR ON A WIRE

"I didn't survive being shot nine times for nothing. I didn't claw my way out of the hood just because it was something to do. I know I've got a purpose – a reason for being on this planet. I don't think I've done everything I'm supposed to do yet. But I do know this: I ain't going nowhere 'til I've done it all."

Curtis James Jackson III

CHAPTER ELEVEN:
The Politics of Testing and Scandal

"Reality has its own power – you can turn your back on it, but it will find you in the end, and your inability to cope with it will be your ruin."

Curtis James Jackson III
The 50th Law

Local leaders across America have played reindeer games with education as well. Details that have emerged over the past decade in the District of Columbia and in neighboring Prince George's County, Maryland, paint portraits of educational reform with seamless similarities of corruption, concealment and collusion. A common cord connects these two school districts – mayoral and county executive oversight. Mayoral oversight has been in place in the District of Columbia since former mayor Adrian M. Fenty named Michelle Rhee his chancellor. Rushern L. Baker, current county executive in Prince George's County, took control of the county's school system in and named Kevin Maxwell his chief executive officer. Rhee left the District once Fenty's re-election bid failed. Vincent Gray named Kaya Henderson, Rhee's deputy chancellor, as his chancellor. When elected as mayor, Muriel Bowser quickly fell into formation by retaining Henderson until circumstances demanded change. Then Bowser chose Antwan Wilson until circumstances forced yet another change in school leadership.

Countless scandals have unfolded in the District of Columbia Public Schools (DCPS) and Prince George's County Public Schools (PGCPS), so many that it's become difficult at times to keep up. Each of the three chancellors in the District over the past decade – Rhee, Henderson and Wilson – own unique scandals. The predominant scandals in

Prince George's County belong mainly to Kevin Maxwell, the current schools chief. Let's begin with the District's scandals.

District of Columbia Public Schools Erasuregate

One of the widest school cheating scandals in American history unfolded in March 2011 when *USA Today* reporters Jack Gillum, Marisol Bello and other colleagues published investigative articles about 103 DCPS schools with significant wrong to right erasures. Some principals and teachers received bonuses and other forms of compensation for questionable test scores. At least one gala held to celebrate teachers, a party that cost almost $750K, celebrated unverified test scores. During this time, I also remember a public relations campaign featuring stories about the test scores. The campaign included signs on city buses, metro stops and billboards featuring selected principals with the twofold purpose of glorifying test scores and recruiting likeminded administrators to the school system.

School Testing Plans

Every school is required in most school districts to submit a formal testing plan. There are state and federal guidelines each local district must meet. These plans outline the specific policies and protocols to be followed during each school's testing period. Each principal chooses a specific testing coordinator. Testing coordinators attend division-wide training during which the school district's central office administrators present testing non-negotiable items, the expectations that must be followed. In turn, the testing coordinator provides training for the faculty, staff, proctors and volunteers. Training includes but is not limited to how tests and answer sheets will be handled, processes and procedures during testing sessions, how the classroom should be set up, which visual aids are to be covered and/or removed, bathroom protocol and the specific duties for the administering teacher or examiner and the proctor, an additional adult assigned to the classroom to ensure honesty and supervision of students during testing. Each school's plan is specific and submitted to the central office for approval. If modifications are needed, they're guided by central office employees. Although this is a concise overview of the testing coordinator's role and the testing plan, it demonstrates there are policies in place for governance and for administering the test.

How Could Cheating Take Place?

Cheating on standardized tests when protocols are properly enforced is next to impossible without collusion and coordination. What most likely happened in the District is much more sinister and complex. Quality school testing plans prohibit all adults except the testing coordinator from having custody of the tests. This means there is too little time for teachers to erase and change multiple student answer sheets from wrong to right without an accomplice. Just as with the scenario of teachers being unable to get away with giving students the answers in front of the class and the proctor, it's highly unlikely this scenario would work.

There are, however, several ways teachers and proctors can bend the rules to increase test scores. One tactic is giving students additional time to complete the test. Standardized tests are timed. A second strategy is providing accommodations, provision normally granted to special education students and students who are enrolled in coursework for English as a second language to further support their academic needs. I recall an incident with one of my teachers at Rudolph Elementary School. He had a profanity-laced tantrum because I refused to allow one of his students to have illegal accommodations to which she wasn't entitled. While I understood his desire to advocate for his student, it was also a part of his responsibility throughout the instructional year to ensure she received services prior to testing to properly prepare for testing prior to receiving test materials. At the same time, I had to respect the rules and respect the integrity of our school's testing plan and test administration. Using these tactics would prevent the affected classes from being a standardized group because all students have to take the test under the same conditions for their scores to be valid.

A third way teachers and proctors influence testing is by reading test questions and student responses under the guise of making sure students are working. This time can be strategically used to advise students to check their responses to certain questions before the testing period ends. During this time, teachers and proctors could also "fat finger" the correct answer for students by placing a finger beside the correct answer, thus leading the student to choose a specific response.

The other means by which school based employees could cheat on standardized tests are much more layered and sinister. One scenario involves "trusted" faculty and staff members who come together for "erasure parties." These erasure parties must include the school's testing coordinator because it is only through the coordinator the trusted group can gain access to testing booklets and answer sheets. The testing coordinator provides free reign and time for the trusted group to erase and change student responses from wrong to right.

Cheating Rationalization

This is a far more logical explanation for the average of ten incorrect responses erased to correct answers as reported by Jay Mathews of the *Washington Post*. In June 2012, when Mathews asked then chancellor Kaya Henderson about students who'd changed high percentages of their responses from wrong to right, Henderson attempted to explain it with her claim that students could have skipped questions and erased them later while checking their work. This could happen among some students but it isn't like to happen simultaneously in 103 schools. My progressive years of experience as a teacher, assistant principal and principal make this a naïve and incredulous explanation.

First, it's a challenge to get most students to review their work during normal circumstances. It's even less likely students carefully review their work during standardized testing unless of prodded by the examiner or proctor. Of course, Henderson's explanation underscores the possibility of students being led to correct responses during the testing period. Second, during testing sessions, if the examiner and proctor are monitoring students as vigilantly as they're supposed to, they will notice if students have made an error before it becomes a page's worth of incorrectly recorded responses. Rumors abound in the District about multiple "erasure parties" to boost schools' test scores. It's also possible the principal and testing coordinator could erase and correct student responses. Remember, principals select their testing coordinators. Naturally, principals choose a person who shares their agenda. There are pervasive rumors about a DCPS principal in particular taking the test sheets and answer keys home and changing them on the kitchen table. That's a smooth way to violate the school's testing plan and boost scores, all with an eraser and a number two pencil.

Under pressure, the District initially hired Caveon, a consulting company, to investigate the scores after *USA Today* exposed the erasure scandal. A second investigation into the 103 schools yielded little substantive data about the erasures. Alvarez and Marsal, a consulting firm DCPS has contracted multiple times to verify its student enrollment count, performed the second inquiry. This inquiry came into question when reporters asked District officials why they ignored the wrong to right erasures that surfaced in 2008 during Rhee's first year as chancellor. The erasures remained concealed quite conveniently since District officials rewrote their own rules to prevent deeper investigations going forward.

Cheating scandals in our schools across the nation are a disgrace to our students and, as did officials in DCPS, they're more often than not swept under the rug. Few school districts face them with the transparency officials in the State of Georgia showed. Cheating allegations during high stakes educational testing became public scandals in Atlanta while District of Columbia Public Schools leaders concealed their cheating allegations beneath several investigations requested by DCPS and OSSE officials to examine suspicious erasures. Had it not been for the poignant, data-rich *USA Today* investigative reporting on DCPS cheating, the suspicious erasures would have remained among the school system's best-kept secrets and lies. It did not serve parents or students in the District well when leaders, both elected and appointed, weren't held accountable. That said, it's difficult to believe any of the results that emerged from the District's cloaked "investigative" efforts are reliable.

Officials in the State of Georgia pursued cheating in Atlanta Public Schools transparently once the scandal spiraled out of the alleged control of Beverly Hall and her comrades. Hall and company faced scrutiny from the Professional Standards Commission that oversees credentialed Georgia educators. Georgian sanctions can be as light as a warning and as consequential as loss of professional licensure. Hall's cheating scandal emerged among 44 schools while Rhee's suspicious erasures involved 103 schools. With over twice the number of schools involved in wrong to right erasures in the District than in Atlanta, let's address the elephant in the room. Why did Hall's misdeeds garner action and consequences while Rhee skipped along without consequences for more than twice the amount of cheating accusations?

Both cheating scandals are similar. Kathy Augustine worked alongside Hall during the alleged tainting of Atlanta schools scores. Kaya Henderson and Michelle Rhee, joined at the hip before they began working in the District, were a team during Rhee's tenure in the District. Henderson, Rhee's former deputy, and also a former chancellor of the District's schools, was present throughout the suspicious erasures. Hall resigned her post by issuing an exhaustive letter simultaneously denying wrongdoing and glorifying her accomplishments. Hall, a highly qualified, credentialed, experienced educator, was silent in her post- Atlanta Public Schools life until she died. Rhee resigned in the weeks after Adrian Fenty lost his mayoral re-election bid to Vincent Gray. Yet Rhee, bipartisan advisor to politicians who once robustly supported her brand of reform, crisscrossed the nation as an erstwhile educational star speaking about her accomplishments, embellishing them to fit each crowd she sought to dazzle. Why the marked difference in treatment for

Hall, a woman Rhee said she admired? Rhee, a woman whose classroom management included taping students' mouths shut while she worked in Baltimore City's Harlem Park Elementary School, used similar strategies with adults given that other than the thorough reporting in *USA Today*, very few people ever became willing to speak up about the cheating scandal.

    Kathy Augustine, Hall's deputy, sailed into a superintendent's position in DeSoto, Texas, a Dallas suburb, but she resigned after one day's work. At the conclusion of an investigation, Augustine received an undisclosed financial settlement from the DeSoto Board of Education when she departed the post. Henderson, Rhee's deputy, dodged accountability and became Rhee's successor. While Augustine, a credentialed, experienced educator, was unable to serve a full term as DeSoto's superintendent because of what happened in Atlanta, Henderson managed to preside over DCPS for almost a decade. Why were outcomes also so vastly different between Augustine and Henderson?

    Next, former Atlanta area superintendents Sharon Davis-Williams, Michael Pitts, Robin Hall and Tamara Cotman faced Georgia sanctions in tandem with Hall and Augustine. In the District, only one instructional superintendent, a principal whom Rhee promoted, has been named in the 103-school scandal. It remains unclear in both of the District's lean and superficial investigations whether this individual is solely alleged a cheater based on accusations of questionable conduct while serving as a principal or after the promotion to instructional superintendent. This begs several questions. Why was this person's name one of the only names to emerge from the DCPS and OSSE investigations? Cheating in a single school as a principal is one matter but cheating across 103 schools is another situation altogether. It is difficult to entertain the notion that only one instructional superintendent became involved in systemic erasures. According to the DCPS website, there were 127 operating schools at the time. How could one person logically be the only alleged middle manager with culpability for suspicious erasures among all but 24 of the District's schools? Did this person simply an inconvenient instructional superintendent?

  Georgia officials remained unwilling to allow their cheating scandal to fester in silence. District City Council members appeared to be content with allowing the sordid mess to remain investigated at the surface. If the majority of District council members and the mayor hadn't so preoccupied with skunks and funks of their own, they would have been less inclined to ignore the elephant in the room. Perhaps at least one council member should have had the courage to demand a genuine investigation to answer the difficult questions that had yet to be addressed.

The public must demand better results and transparency. The people in the District deserved an equally honest, robust investigation like the one in Atlanta. Georgia officials provided answers about *who* orchestrated the cheating and *how* the cheating took place. Parents and students in the District deserved no less. Justice indeed costs. Almost a decade later, the question still remains. Who, in this case, covered the costs for Rhee's cheating scandal?

While Michelle Rhee and Kaya Henderson share ownership of the wide-spread DCPS erasure scandal, Henderson uniquely owns scandals of her own. When she separated from DCPS, Henderson left behind an academic achievement gap, in some cases an even wider achievement gap among black and white students. Multiple media outlets reported Henderson's actions, yet nothing was done about them until Mayor Bowser's hand was forced to deal with the situation.

Henderson and the Lottery System

DCPS has a lottery system in place to guarantee fairness with out of boundary transfers. Henderson overrode the District's lottery system when, as disclosed by the District of Columbia Inspector General, she used her position as chancellor to provide multiple people preferential school placements for their children. Those who received special treatment included one Obama White House staff member, two of Bowser's mayoral appointees, a former District elected official, a nonprofit head in partnership with the school district, one DCPS principal and one of Henderson's alumni associates. As the District's mayor, Bowser reportedly exerted no effort to find out which of appointees sought special favors. In fact, Bowser's spokesperson deflected from the appointees' accepting special favors by blaming Henderson for misusing her power, all the while ignoring the fact Bowser's appointees sought preferential treatment in the first place.

Show Henderson the Money

Henderson's most serious misstep occurred when she solicited donations from city contractors to underwrite costs for a gala in honor of teachers. In 2016, Henderson solicited $100K from Chartwells, the school system's food services vendor. According to multiple media reports, Henderson committed further acts of graft when she sought and accepted similar donations from other District contractors, including $25K from Thompson Hospitality, Chartwells catering division. Henderson sought and accepted two $25K donations from Chartwells. Henderson solicited funds from other city vendors as well, including Sodexo, one of the other vendors bidding on the city's food services contract at the time.

Henderson feigned innocence, claiming she didn't know her actions had been inappropriate. It's difficult to believe Henderson's protests of ignorance given that city leaders receive annual ethics training. Soliciting money from city contractors can and should be considered corruption of the contracting process because doing so can be construed as a pay to play scenario. Given that she sought donations from Chartwells, then the food services contractor and one of its competitors in the contracting process, Sodexo, Henderson's actions are a clear conflict of interest and appear on their face as quid pro quos for donations in exchange for consideration on the contracts.

What makes Henderson's actions further disturbing is that her appeal to Chartwells for funds came after the city settled a whistleblower's suit in 2014. The whistleblower, who Henderson fired, won a $450K settlement from the District. The lawsuit came about because of acts of fraud, price gouging and accusations that Chartwells provided spoiled meals to the District's children after hoarding food they deliberately allowed to spoil. Despite their egregious and greedy actions that endangered children with putrid meals, the Council of the District of Columbia allowed Chartwells to continue serving its children meals with a $32 million contract the next year.

Bowser appeared unbothered about two breaches of public trust, one matter that had roots in her office. First, Bowser's spokesperson scapegoated Henderson for granting the special favors her appointees and others asked for. Next, after being placed in an intractable position, Bowser allowed Henderson to resign without holding her accountable for soliciting donations and possible contract tampering, a clear violation of the Government of the District of Columbia ethics. Once public attention focused on both of the scandals, Bowser made an independent move by choosing Antwan Wilson as her administration's chancellor.

Wilson at the Helm

In a little less than a year, Wilson weathered two major scandals. First, there were the grade inflations and padded attendance records for Ballou High School seniors. Second, there is Wilson's abuse of the boundary transfer policies and procedures that benefitted his daughter.

You Get a Diploma, Everyone Gets a Diploma

In 2016, another scandal emerged in DCPS, a graduation scandal that created another historic moment for the District's schools. Ballou High School graduated 164 students, all of whom gained accepted to college. This historic moment garnered publicity from every corner of the nation. Yet, behind the magic, pomp and circumstance, Ballou's faculty and staff questioned how this victorious moment came to pass. American University radio station WAMU and National Public Radio (NPR) conducted an investigation and their findings, both disturbing and troublesome, shed light on the situation. Their investigation yielded results that are statistically rich and quite telling.

Many of the students who graduated missed more than three months of school. Three months equal approximately ninety days, two marking periods in most school districts, including DCPS. The District's attendance policy states that if students miss a class thirty times, they fail the course. To have thirty absences, nearly a full marking period, and receive a passing grade is quite liberal. How did students with such excessive absences legally graduate?

Ballou faculty and staff members admitted the administration exerted pressure on them for students to graduate. The investigation results indicate that some teachers received requests to change students' grades. They were asked to assign make up work and to provide extra credit assignments, among other strategies. Extra credit is typically additional work for students who've already met the baseline expectations. It's difficult to earn extra credit when you haven't earned baseline credits. Ballou administrators also implemented a program called credit recovery. This program allows students to attend accelerated versions of courses they're already failing for a few weeks after hours. Credit recovery courses aren't as intense as the daily classes and appear to be a means to push students out of school. When they refused, teachers said they were punitively given unsatisfactory evaluations if they refused to play by the administration's rules.

    Doing as an administrator asks can serve teachers in several ways. First, teachers are able to keep their jobs and support themselves and their families. Second, they along with their administrators, can earn bonuses from the school district for increased test scores. Of the 164 students who graduated, only 57% met graduation requirements. The remaining 107 did not meet mandated requirements. They didn't earn passing grades, meet attendance requirements or complete their community service requirements.

    When asked about the Ballou graduation scandal, Mayor Bowser deferred to Wilson, then the DCPS chancellor and Jane Spence, the DCPS Chief of Secondary Schools. Yetunde Reeves, then Ballou's principal, declined the opportunity to share her side of the story. Wilson responded by elaborating on the stressors the District's students experience in their personal lives. While it's a fact many of the students live challenging lives, it's the school system's responsibility to provide public education opportunities to better equip them to deal with these challenges and prepare them to lead better lives in the future. There has to be a better way to support our students on the path to success than pushing them through school just to say they graduated.

Jane Spence also discussed the challenges DCPS students experience and praised the credit recovery program and make up assignments as viable approaches. She also attempted to explain her position by pointing out the differences between school absences and class absences, asserting that it's possible for students to have thirty days of absences without thirty absences from a particular class. It's difficult to rationalize this interpretation. If a student misses thirty days of school, he or she conceivably missed thirty days of coursework. At the point the interviewer asked Wilson and Spence how the students graduated, they quickly ended the interview. The question has yet to be answered.

Love Knows No Boundary

Abuse of the school boundary transfer process is a recurring scandal the District has been unable to avoid in recent years. While Kaya Henderson was proverbially slapped on the wrist for accommodating a list of high profile appointees and officials, Wilson's sidestep around the policy ultimately cost two officials their appointments. Wilson sought assistance for his daughter's transfer to Wilson High School over their neighborhood school, Dunbar High School, from Jennifer Niles, the Deputy Mayor for Education.

On one hand, Wilson did what any concerned father would do in advocating for his daughter. No one can fault a father for that. On the other hand, Wilson did not go to Niles directly. Instead, Wilson's wife spoke to Niles. After their conversation, Niles facilitated the transfer, giving Wilson's daughter the transfer that hundreds of other students' parents requested previously to the Wilsons. The fact that Mrs. Wilson served as a proxy for her husband doesn't make the act of favoritism no less problematic. In fact, it can be viewed as Wilson distancing himself from the request to avoid public scrutiny.

Wilson violated the very policy he rewrote when responding to the Henderson transfer scandal. Wilson revised the policy when Bowser directed him to do so likely in part because some of Bowser's appointees benefitted from

Henderson bending the rules in their favor. Three months after revising the policy, Wilson violated it.

After his departure, Wilson shared with the media that he told Bowser in October his daughter had transferred to Wilson High School. Four months later, Bowser forced him to resign his post once the public became aware of Niles' and Wilson's actions favoring his daughter. Reports have emerged that Wilson's resignation happened in order to protect Bowser's image. She's seeking reelection and, amidst enrollment fraud at other District schools and a federal probe into inflated graduation rates among multiple District high schools, it is no wonder Bowser would be concerned about her image. She has spun the issue by solely blaming Niles and Wilson for the transfer and is conveniently unable to recall whether Wilson told her about the transfer. Wilson said Bowser asked him about his family and how his daughter was doing at Wilson. With all bases covered, we'll possibly never know what really happened.

Prince George's County Public Schools Scandals

Prince George's County, a stone's throw from the District, has its similar challenges. Over the past five years, Kevin Maxwell has had his fair share of scandals. He spent a large portion of the school system's budget to add to the bloat of central office staff, so many the school system had to add a new telephone exchange to accommodate the extra employees. Much of the money spent on the salaries and benefits for excessive central office staffing would be better spent on school based needs, such as academic intervention for early childhood students, placing a fulltime media specialist in each school, additional STEM teachers, expanded capital improvement or other instructional additions to narrow the county's academic achievement gap.

Down Goes Head Start

It's especially critical that Prince George's County officials invest more local funds in academic intervention for early childhood students because the school system lost its $6.5 million Head Start grant in 2016. Among most county families, many low income families in particular depend on Head Start to provide early academic opportunities for their children. A vital Head Start program can diminish and in some cases eliminate the achievement gap among low, middle and upper class students. Prince George's County Public Schools lost its Head Start Program because central office employees failed to address and correct deficiencies they had been made aware of through an official internal audit and accountability report in December 2015. Segun Eubanks, the appointed school board chair, received the report. Among the most alarming deficiencies the school system failed to address are documented incidents of corporal punishment and physical abuse and an unsupervised child left unattended who wandered away from the building.

Three specific examples of the school system's failure to take corrective action with come to mind. When I read the report detailing these incidents, I became incensed as an educator.

Accidents Happen

During an incident in December 2015, at H. Winship Wheatley Early Childhood Education Center, a teacher made one of her three-year old students clean his urine after he had an accident during naptime. As the child cleaned up the spill, the teacher took photographs. Afterward, the teacher humiliated the child by forcing him to stand in front of the classroom while wearing his urine stained clothing. Next, the teacher texted the child's mother the photographs with comments that included LOL (Laughing Out Loud) and "He worked that mop, tho." As any parent would be, the little boy's mother, upset and angry about how her child had been treated, reported her concerns about the teacher. The audit report indicates attempts made to talk the mother out of pursuing the matter.

A month later in January 2016, the mother followed her instincts and formally reported the incident. Instead of following the legal reporting mandate to either Child Services or the police department, the incident remained concealed, reported only through an internal email to the principal and program director.

Determined to receive justice for her child, the mother sent an email including the teacher's photographs and texts to Dr. Maxwell and Instructional Director Judith White, among other executive level employees. Only then were the appropriate procedures followed with a report to Child Protective Services, eight days later than legally required.

During a news conference with WUSA 9, Maxwell said the teacher was immediately removed from the Head Start Program. He failed to mention the teacher had been transferred to another school and was working with other children, all despite the fact federal investigators investigated and proved the allegations of abuse and bullying against her. After being placed on administrative leave for a second time, this teacher was recommended to be fired.

Naptime at James Ryder Randall Elementary School

During this incident in June 2016, two children behaved mischievously during nap time. Their teachers collectively punished them by making them hold heavy items over their heads until they were allowed to stop. When the children began crying and repeatedly calling the teachers' names, the teachers ignored them.

Home Alone

A third child, this time a five year old, left the Langley Park Head Start center unsupervised and walked home alone in June 2016. After going to see the school nurse, the child left the school building unnoticed. A family member found the unattended child waiting outside of the apartment building where she lived.

In both incidents of corporal punishment, the punishments were not age-appropriate. It was unnecessary to humiliate three year olds for having an accident and behaving mischievously. For a five year old to be able to leave the school building without anyone noticing and walking home alone is completely frightening and unacceptable. In most schools, younger children are sent to the office, the school nurse and other destinations outside of the classroom on a buddy system so they aren't alone.

In a very politically shrewd manner, school system officials informed their stakeholders the Head Start program would close. When informing everyone, the school system never owned its role in the situation. Not one member of Maxwell's team, despite the fact these kinds of audit findings are public, took accountability for failing to address the program's deficiencies. Moving forward a year later when the truth of the scandal finally came to light, the person who appears to have managed the Head Start scandal for Maxwell, former Chief of Staff George Margolies, tried to prevent the news from becoming public.

A spirited exchange of emails between Margolies and school board vice chair Carolyn Boston emerged in April 2016, painting a vivid portrait of how desperately Maxwell appears to have wanted to contain the Head Start debacle. According to the emails, Boston struck a deal with Margolies not to include the Head Start as an item on the board of education's official agenda. Via email, Margolies reassured a deputy superintendent the item had been blocked once he and Boston had brokered the deal. Vice Chair Boston also admitted she and Margolies have differing views on what the board of education as a whole should know and discuss. Board of Education members are elected to set and enforce policies, not to defer to the chief executive officer or his designees. As the vice chair, Boston must remember several things. First, the board of education supervises the chief executive officer. Second, the chair and vice chair do not have the right to prevent their colleagues from having equal access to news about the school system. When the deal came to light, Maxwell denied it, explaining it away as a tactic not to overload the Board's agenda. Board Chair Segun Eubanks, the member most responsible for setting the Board's agenda, later said the Board had been briefed on Head Start issues during one of its private sessions, a session some members chose not to attend. Given that private sessions are closed, the public will never know the full truth.

Once news about the Head Start scandal broke to the public and the rest of the board of education, Margolies' time as chief of staff ended. According to media reports, it appears Margolies fell on his sword for Maxwell in September 2016. After serving Maxwell since December 2013, Margolies resigned when Maxwell apparently asked him to.

The Head Start scandal could have been an easy fix had it been handled promptly and transparently. Policies and procedures exist to handle incidents of corporal punishment and other deficiencies detailed in the December 2015 accountability report. Had the incident been handled properly, the county's children would still reap the benefits of the Head Start program. Yet, the school system's leadership failed to take the required steps to address the deficiencies listed in the accountability report. Instead, they chose to replace the amount of money needed to salvage the program and their reputations in the meantime rather than considering the long-term value of early academic intervention and holding themselves accountable for poor governance and their failure to make quality, transparent change. As a school system already engaged in battle against a socioeconomic achievement gap, it's baffling how they failed to grasp the importance of maintaining a Head Start program for the students.

Child Abuse Wasn't Unique to Head Start

Sadly, other scandals involving the abuse of children have emerged on Maxwell's watch. According to media reports, on September 1, 2016, a private nurse boarded one of the school buses at C. Elizabeth Rieg Regional School and physically assaulted an autistic student with her fists and one of her shoes after she became frustrated because the student was poking her. No one asked this individual for identification before she boarded the bus. No one did anything to prevent her from approaching the student. On September 14, 2016, two weeks *after* the assault, Maxwell viewed the assault. The day after Maxwell's viewing, Prince

George's County Public Schools investigators finally received notice the assault occurred.

James Ryder Randall Elementary School

Several weeks *before* the assault at C. Elizabeth Rieg, media reports indicate a school bus aide had been accused of molesting a four year old special needs student on the bus to and from James Ryder Randall Elementary School. When this child's parents found out their baseline expectation of and right to safety for their child had been violated, Maxwell stated that the school system had turned the incident over to the police department and that if law enforcement hadn't contacted them, there was no need for worry. Maxwell, deflecting from this incident, revealed the principal from Judge Sylvania Woods Elementary School had been placed on administrative leave without disclosing a reason for the situation.

Judge Sylvania Woods Elementary School

Maxwell's statement about the second principal and incident at Judge Sylvania Woods Elementary School infuriated school board member Edward Burroughs. Burroughs shared during an executive board session with

Maxwell that neither of these incidents had been shared with the Board of Education. Maxwell mentioned this second incident during a press conference as a deflection from the James Ryder Randall bus abuse incident. His deflection from this incident came a year *after* the principal had been replaced at Judge Sylvania Woods when a school volunteer sexually abused students. Allegations against the volunteer include coercing children into performing sexual acts that he filmed on his cell phone, thus creating child pornography. Some of his victims, totaling almost twenty children according to some sources, were as young as nine years old.

System Wide High School Grade and Attendance Scandal

As if these incidents and the many that haven't publicly surfaced aren't alarming enough, PGCPS scandals don't stop there. The grade and attendance scandal is a grand embarrassing mess that could have been mitigated and resolved several years before it exploded. An internal audit in 2016 revealed grade and attendance tampering, yet Maxwell and board of education chairperson Segun Eubanks once again failed to tangibly intervene and they concealed the audit's findings. Further, it's unclear whether and when Eubanks shared the report with the school board as a whole before this scandal also became public. Most disturbingly, it appears nothing of consequence was done about it until four board of education members contacted the Maryland Governor's office to request a state audit.

Rationalize, Squash, Conceal and Deflect

Maxwell's actions to rationalize and squash the scandal coupled with Eubanks' inaction in response to this latest in a series of scandals are a disappointing, disturbing trend. First, Maxwell denied the concerns about grade and attendance falsification in spite of the fact he had been made aware of the inconsistencies two years before the state's audit. Once the four Board members requested the state audit, Maxwell tried to deflect from the cheating scandal by accusing those who requested the audit of making him a political target, this as he continued to defend county graduation rates all the while definitely aware of the internal audit's findings that proved otherwise. His third tactic in August emerged when he referred to the allegations as rash. Upon the release of the state audit findings, Maxwell changed his tune once again, this time calling the state audit's findings a scheme to challenge his leadership instead of a means to improve the school system.

Soon after Maxwell's next waffle in response to the scandal, he said during a school board meeting he'd delegated others on his vast central office staff to respond to the audit. Essentially, this appears to be an excuse that the school system is too vast for him to manage every detail, despite the fact he decided to expand it. It isn't difficult to review and improve upon details in an internal audit report, though it is an established practice of his to do so.

None of Maxwell's explanations mitigate the conscious decision he made to celebrate graduation rates he knew to be inaccurate with a surprise bus tour of schools. Amidst the cheering, dancing in the hallways and pop-up bus rides and celebrations, Maxwell had full knowledge of every irregularity reported in the 2016 internal audit. Yet, he chose to celebrate the irregularities anyway. With every step he took, every word he uttered, every boastful statement he made and every smile he flashed for the cameras and audiences, he knew and consciously chose to brag about tainted grades, falsified attendance records and inaccurate graduation rates. Amidst the deception, fraud, trickery and lies, Maxwell chose to celebrate it all.

Board of Education chairperson Eubanks channeled Maxwell's sentiments with his attempt to distract attention from the state audit's validity. Eubanks sought to circle the wagons with the sentiment that the issues addressed in the state audit should've been addressed at the local level. This is puzzling. Eubanks had an opportunity to address the internal audit at the local level in 2016, yet he remained silent. Eubanks' role in the scandal is problematic for numerous reasons.

First, Eubanks received his appointment as Board Chair from his former brother-in-law, Rushern Baker. The county executive's governance over the school system allows him to choose the chair. The relationship between Baker and Eubanks is a potential ethical dilemma given the amount of power and influence Eubanks wields as a result of his appointment. Baker supervises Eubanks who supervises Maxwell. This dynamic should cause concern. Prior to his appointment and until his recent appointment, Eubanks worked for the National Educators Association (NEA), the national teacher's union. While working for the NEA and serving as the board's chair, Eubanks sat in judgment over contracts for the local teachers union, a chapter that is a part of the NEA. He also presided over and made key decisions about the other labor unions' contracts as well.

Second, after he retired from the NEA, Eubanks started a position at the University of Maryland. Eubanks' newest day job is coincidentally the former position held by Donna Wiseman, one of the most recently appointed board of education members. His newest employment opportunity and the new board member's appointment are intriguingly opportune and could also pose an ethical concern.

Third, Eubanks' responsibility is to work for the students and families he serves and to articulate and enforce board policies and procedures, not to circle the wagons for Maxwell. Eubanks and the other Board of Education members, whether elected and appointed, are supposed to supervise Maxwell, not defend or represent him. Eubanks' criticism of the audit is essentially tantamount to referring to four of his colleagues as "snitches." Eubanks complained that people in the school system went to the Governor and made the audit happen rather than working within the school system to resolve the matter. Had the four board members not contacted the Governor, Eubanks and Maxwell likely would've continued burying the internal audit that they had nearly eighteen months prior to the state audit. The lines have been blurred and Eubanks appears more invested in protecting Maxwell and Baker's interests than he is in upholding his duties as the chair of the board of education.

Two Audits, Similar Results

Findings from the state audit cannot be silenced as was the May 2016 internal audit. The state audit validates and broadens the deficiencies exposed at the local level that Maxwell justified before throwing some of his own staff under the bus, the same report Eubanks never bothered to disclose to or discuss with the board of education as he should have as board chair. The state audit findings are brutal. The report documented the local inconsistencies and failures with the school system's failure to monitor its grading policies and procedures. Some students' grades were submitted and changed after grading periods ended. Staff members other than the students' teachers changed grades, changes most of the teachers were unaware of. Personnel overlooked grade change justification forms. Reports emerged that some guidance counselors passed around lists of students who needed assistance to graduate. The audit's findings suggest that PGCPS used social promotion to graduate students with deficient skills, essentially pushing them out of the school.

 Statistics gathered in the state audit validate the findings. According to the state audit report, the state examined approximately 1200 student records out of a cumulative 5,496 students who "graduated" from PGCPS in 2016 and 2017. The percentages, grim and disappointing, are as follows:

> 43.8% of the examined students graduated despite having more than ten unexcused absences,
> 24.5% of "graduates" in 2016 and 2017 received improper grade changes.

4.9% of the students were completely ineligible to graduate even with inappropriate grade changes. Many of the students included in this percentage received grade changes *after* their graduation ceremonies.

Statistics summarized, one of four students in Prince George's County in 2016 and 2017, possible in earlier years also given the brazen actions described in the audit, who graduated did not fulfill any of their graduation requirements. The graduates who've been pushed out of Prince George's County and the District have been harmed by the choices some very selfish adults made for ambition, recognition, bonuses and accolades, others out of fear and desperate to keep their jobs. Unfortunately, these students aren't the only ones who've been harmed by high stakes testing and cheating. It's happening all over the nation but these are the examples with which I'm most familiar.

CHAPTER TWELVE:
There's No One in Charge

"We need to steer clear of this poverty of ambition, where people want to drive fancy cars and wear nice clothes and live in nice apartments but don't want to work hard to accomplish these things. Everyone should try to realize their full potential."

President Barack Obama

The myriad scandals we just discussed represent the gold plated brick road leading our students to the precipice of a poverty of testing through cheating and over-testing. My experiences, accomplishments and memories as an educator reinvigorated within me a need to choose defiance in the wake of educational injustice and scandals and the socioeconomic and political miseducation being thrust upon our children. It's time to say no to this testing agenda against our children and to say yes to first instilling in our children the value and importance of earning a quality education. Our students have diverse needs and we are ignoring too many of those needs because they're not a testing objective. This agenda of overemphasizing standardized testing has created a chasm in American education. It's time to build a bridge of balance across this chasm.

So many American students have innate talent and interest in vocational expertise like plumbing, HVAC, brick masonry and so forth; yet, so many of our school districts are ignoring and marginalizing these talents. It is equally ludicrous to downplay a student's natural talents in order to promote the belief that all students should attend college. We could boost our economy with a diverse pool of graduates that includes those with highly skilled trades, students who will join the armed forces and college bound high school graduates. We should function as a diverse society, not one that produces cookie cutter students who don't enjoy the freedom to follow their own aspirations. In America, everyone is supposed to have the opportunity to become what he or she wants to be. While this sounds like a naïve philosophy to many, as an experienced educator, I've noticed a shift from a student-oriented focus to a political focus, a shift that has done much more harm than good for our students.

While I believe assessment is necessary and avail means to use in determining how well we're educating our children, assessment cannot and should not ever replace learning. We shouldn't aim to create students who can regurgitate facts for a test. Instead, we must prepare students can think for themselves, form intelligent, divergent opinions and who can contribute to society. Instead, we've made end of year tests the pinnacle of educational accomplishment while creating students who are bored and much less enthusiastic than they should be.

This myopic focus on testing has also created an inordinate amount of pressure for teachers, principals, our children and some central office personnel. Teachers are expected to create miracles among their students while enduring covert and overt pressures to increase test scores and narrow the achievement gap by any means necessary.

While being pushed to teach to the test, teachers are managing classrooms with students who have deeper academic, social and emotional needs, some of which are so deeply rooted that the teachers feel the pressure and it becomes virtually impossible for some of the students to cope. These dilemmas cause our teachers to step into the roles of surrogate parent. They often purchase additional classroom and individual supplies for students with personal funds.

They often act as social workers while helping families that need additional support. Psychologist is another role many teachers take on when they're working with students and trying to diagnose learning or emotional disabilities. Navigating the child study process in most school districts is difficult and tedious at best. It become another instructional stressor when students who need additional support don't qualify for additional services because they fell slightly out of range and didn't meet the criteria or numbers for assistance.

Far too many American teachers are judged by and evaluated according to their students' test scores. When students are struggling in their classes and expecting stressful situations at home, teachers are still expected to prepare these students to pass an end of year test. In some cases, this is next to impossible. In other cases, when students can be prepared adequately to pass the test, how helpful is the knowledge they've acquired when it's at recall level to record on a bubble sheet? When these students move to the next grade level or course, they are often further behind academically. Through each year, as the cycle continues, the achievement gap widens and continues, trapping some of the students in cyclical failure.

Think of the stressors we discussed our teachers and principals face. A classic example is middle school student Randy Wagstaff during Season Four of *The Wire*. Randy, an intelligent fifteen year old, was exploited and devoured by the system. A foster child, Randy remained resilient, using his entrepreneurial gift quickly to earn money by selling candy and snacks to schoolmates. A mischievous and fast thinking boy, Randy became trapped in crossfire between his assistant principal and the police department when he disclosed his knowledge of a homicide in order to get out of trouble at school. Once his assistant principal notified the police about what Randy told her, Randy's stressors intensified.

Detective Hauk, one of the less thinking detectives, unwittingly revealed Randy's identify to one of his informants who in turn reported the incident to his drug crew. Labeled a snitch on the streets once word reached Marlo Stanfield, the predatory drug lord who ordered the murder, Randy's home burned down in an act of arson that severely injured his foster mother and left Randy homeless.

Sgt. Carver, an officer familiar with Randy who had become more sensitive to the needs of the community, intervened to help Randy as requested by his commanding officer. Unsuccessful, even after offering himself as a foster parent, Carver is forced to deliver Randy to a group home. His reputation as a "snitch" preceding him, Randy's life began a downward spiral.

More of our teachers encounter students like Randy than you'd expect. Randy and students like him live challenging lies. We cannot simply sweet their home lives under the rug. We must establish a renewed focus on educating our children rather than merely preparing them to perform well on a test. Providing a solid, quality education is one of the best strategies to level the playing field and truly make America great again.

Teachers in schools where socioeconomically empowered parents enroll their children sometimes make decisions or take actions that cause principals angst. When connected parents are angry about a disciplinary decision or grade, they often call politicians or other influential people to fight their battles for them if they haven't achieve the results they've demanded at the school level rather than working with the principal or the teacher. This also happens often among parents who are frustrated when their children are consistently disruptive or struggling academically. It's often the teacher they lash out against when they feel overwhelmed and don't know what to do. When the principal supports the teacher's actions, it can mushroom into an even bigger concern for the principal who then has to resolve the conflict between the teacher and parents in order to best serve the student.

Here's where the pressures facing school based administrators come into play. Principals are held accountable for virtually everything that happens in their schools. In that regard, principals are the truest middle managers. Principals balance multiple responsibilities. In their schools, above all else, they're held accountable for increasing test scores, all too often through veiled threats of demotion and firings. Principals are required to maintain a safe and orderly learning environment, ensure that teachers and assistant principals follow the curriculum as designated by the school system with special attention to and focus on testing goals and they have deadlines to regularly observe and evaluate their faculty and staff. They also respond to unanticipated incidents throughout the school day, troubleshoot emergencies and resolve conflicts for parents, school partners and among faculty and staff members.

While balancing these duties at the school level, principals spend a high volume of time assuring their assistant superintendents that testing goals will be met, preparing for regional visits with assistant superintendents and their staffs and putting out fires after parents or faculty and staff forward concerns for which they're seeking alternate resolutions. Principals also receive direction, changes in policy and procedure and at times unsolicited interference from assistant superintendents. The assistant superintendent can become an added burden to the principal, depending on the opinion the assistant superintendent forms and how he or she chooses to use the incident moving forward.

For example, community stakeholders often exert pressure against principals through assistant superintendents if the principal refuses to give them what they want. In some cases, disgruntled community stakeholders escalate calls to the media about issues that could and should be resolved at the school level. Given the current trend toward social media as bona fide news reports, a community stakeholder can exert influence over a school when the assistant superintendent is more motivated to play a political role and save face rather than protecting the integrity of the school instructional program and a solid educational day.

Assistant superintendents wield inordinate amounts of power as granted by their superintendents. As the eyes and ears of their superintendents, they face mandates to increase test scores and to be sure the images of their schools are pristine and press-ready. Assistant superintendents have definitely become more political than instructional in recent years, a trend among many that has damaged more than helped our students, teachers and school based administrators.

The superintendent's agenda and character determines the quality and actions of assistant superintendents. Superintendents working under the supervision of a school board often have different goals and direction than do superintendents who answer solely to locally elected officials with mayoral or county executive control.

End of year testing, while necessary, has made educating our youth a much more adversarial process, particularly since 2007. Too many superintendents and assistant superintendents use quasi Wall Street tactics to appear in full control of their school divisions. Charm is always deployed publicly, especially with the press. As long as you see things their way, you see their charm and affability. When principals' schools aren't making proficient end of year test scores, some assistant superintendents and superintendents become much less charming. Assistant superintendents take their orders from superintendents who take their directives from elected officials, people typically driven by appearances and numbers and invested in maintaining the status quo.

The Wire has another scene that perfectly depicts the manner in which principals are so often threatened with demotion and termination if they don't produce dramatic increases in test scores. During Season Three, commanders attended mandatory Com Stat meetings. During one of the livelier scenes, Bill Rawls, the colonel of the police department, told the district commanders they were expected to maintain a final murder rate of 275 and reduce felony rates by five percent. Rawls told the beleaguered group, "There is no excuse I will accept. I don't care how you do it. Just fucking do it." Burrell, the acting police commissioner, backed Rawls by saying anyone could be removed. Burrell told the group, "You will shut up and step up."

I've been in meetings and conferences much like these as an educator. Many people are afraid to admit they've been spoken to this way or witnessed other people being bullied in such a manner. I'm not. It happened to me and other professionals I know. This culture of intimidation must stop. It's counterproductive and does nothing to improve instruction or educational services for our children.

I've worked as a teacher, assistant principal and principal under various superintendents. I've also served as an adjunct instructor at the university level. Never did I face overwhelming negative overt pressures as an administrator until our schools took on a laser focus on testing rather than educating our children. An exchange between Bumpy Johnson and Frank Lucas during the blockbuster motion picture *American Gangster* reminds me of so many of experiences as a school based leader. It accurately parallels the state of affairs in the District of Columbia, Prince George's County, Maryland, and countless other communities across the nation at present. Waxing philosophically with Frank in an electronics store, Bumpy laments the changes he sees happening around him in Harlem. Corporations like McDonald's began replacing locally owned mom and pop shops. Name brands and big business practices steamrolled what had traditionally been the unique flavor of Harlem. Saddened by the changing landscape, Bumpy noted the emerging lack of ownership and personal service fading in a world of mass production. Bumpy believed there was no apparent concern about the effects on the community along with diminished product quality and lack of uniqueness.

Bumpy said, "You can't find the heart of anything to stick the knife." Before succumbing to his heart attack, Bumpy told Frank to stop calling for help when he realized the economic development changes and gentrification he saw unfolding before him was inevitable. Bumpy realized no one was in charge.

Changing the economic and gentrification patterns he observed wasn't within Bumpy's grasp, though he had been wise enough to observe them and would have made the necessary adjustments had he survived. The educational trends of over-testing and the accompanying watering down of our curricula and cheating scandals, however, are within our power to change. We can no longer allow local leaders to dodge or deflect the responsibilities we've elected them to fulfill. We cannot afford to damage or lose our most precious resource, our youth. It's time for our schools to educate students and provide a place for them to develop their unique talents, learn and build bright, sustainable futures. It's time to choose defiance and take a stand for our children, for our futures, for our nation.

PART FOUR: MADE WHOLE

"Look way deep inside yourself,
Discover the diamond inside, find ya wealth
Once you get it, you gotta live it to the limit."

Nasir Jones,
"Find Ya Wealth"

CHAPTER THIRTEEN:
Lessons Learned

"Even the worst shit that happens to you can be converted into gold if you are clever enough. Every negative is a positive. The bad things that happen to me, I somehow make them good. That means you can't do anything to hurt me."

Curtis James Jackson III

Until the frightening events and unceremonious school closure sharply punctuated my life, my job had become the sum total of my existence. Now I live by seven lessons that provide a strong foundation for my life. This sad event and all of the factors that caused it became catalysts for my growth that reminded me my purpose is a lifelong plan, not any of the degrees I've earned or jobs I've held. Our jobs and the purpose we've each been assigned are not always intertwined. The jobs we have are awarded by people. They're how we support ourselves and those we love but our purpose is something completely different. The purpose we receive is a lifelong mission we are specifically created, prepared and qualified to fulfill.

My focus on my job became singular and myopic, almost overtaking my identity. I used my job to avoid facing and dealing with the pain of so many challenges I didn't want to confront. I focused on my job to deflect rather than believing my faith would carry me through any situation. My ex-husband's betrayal with another woman and the child he conceived with her outside of our marriage and the shame of our subsequent divorce so he could marry the other woman pierced my heart. Throughout this stressful time I became very depressed. I relied on sugary foods and time alone, hiding from the pain in an effort to dull the rejection and pain I felt. At the same time, I buried my disappointments deeply within a determination to become a district level school administrator just like my Soror Martha, one of my mentors, my godmother and my mother's best friend.

After a seven year period of unemployment and all of the challenges and fears that accompany a prolonged trial, I'm reminded each day Who my Source is. It's God. He's kept me, sustained and provided for me in situations I could never survive alone. It wasn't His plan for me to become a district administrator right after leaving Charlotte-Mecklenburg Schools but I don't believe it means I'm not supposed to be an educator. I believe it means He wanted me to learn from and use my experiences and my truth to help others who've experienced trauma and to help enhance public education opportunities and services for American children and educators. I believe I am purposed to be an educator and encourager despite my own mistakes so no matter what happens, I might have lost a job and a few other things BUT *no one* can steal my purpose.

God has a special purpose for you too, a particular mission only you can accomplish. You might lose a job, an opportunity or the person you believed to be the love of your life but rest assured, whatever is purposed for your life won't elude you. No matter what happens, no one can steal or change your purpose.

A second valuable lesson I learned is to always walk in my truth no matter how painful it is. Oprah Winfrey's dramatic Golden Globes speech reinforced my courage and determination to speak my truth. As she so eloquently stated, "What I know for sure is that speaking your truth is the most powerful tool we all have and I'm especially proud and inspired by all the women who have felt strong enough and empowered enough to speak up and share their personal stories. But it's not just a story affecting the entertainment industry, it's one that transcends any culture, geography, race, religion, politics or workplace." Oprah's statement completely reflects how I feel about my learning experiences and about speaking my story, my truth, and my reality.

Life has become much more beautiful and intensely meaningful because I no longer feel the pressure to prove myself to or impress anyone. It doesn't matter whether or not anyone believes I've suffered through a traumatic experience. The fact is, I did. I experienced police intimidation and harassment that has forever changed my life. It's my truth and I'm sharing it because people must realize police abuse doesn't begin with the senseless murders of victims like Jordan Edwards, Sandra Bland, Alton Sterling, Dontre Hamilton, Philando Castille and all of the other tragic, senseless deaths. Police abuse of power, intimidation and harassment begins with the nonphysical incidents like hateful, prolonged traffic stops, selective enforcement and escalates with incidents like pulling strings to entrap citizens, inflicting physical harm and ultimately, murder.

Corruption and abuse of power among elected officials and government leaders is nothing new either. The major difference is that leaders in contemporary times are unapologetically brazen with their power plays. They flout their power recklessly as badges of honor without regard to the collateral damage in the wake of their schemes. I've survived and thrived despite every incident of intimidation, harassment, blackballing and oppression school systems and the police department joined forces to hurl at me. The things that happened to me clandestinely are also my truth. It's became increasingly difficult to fathom and believe a police chief would so carelessly collude with the head of a school system to direct me to participate in an Internal Affairs Division investigation, a disclosure that violated my right to privacy and department policies and procedures. Yet she did. My next truth is a nightmare. It became even more painful to accept that only two brief months after my school had been approved and funded for renovation that its future would be undone because I refused to follow a directive neither the Police Chief nor Chancellor had the grounds or authority to give.

Certainly what happened to me was a forbidding experience and tragically, the effects on my students, their parents and the faculty-staff became intertwined with mine. We'd spent three years improving academic achievement, our school climate and building the greater resources our students so desperately needed that our budget could not and central office officials would not provide. We received books through community donations so our students would have a school library after almost a decade of not having one. We didn't have a sufficient internet server to provide computer time for our student. This negatively affected daily instruction and test preparation activities. Our most generous business partners purchased an independent server and fifty computers for our students and faculty-staff. Six months later, the Chancellor made the capricious decision to close our school.

Their parents, many of whom attended our school as children, felt the effects of the ill advised decision. Once the administration forced our students out of their school home, their parents had to take on the burden of finding another school for them to attend. This meant some of the children had to leave public school and every familiar adult in their daily support system.

The faculty and staff also suffered in the wake of the school closure. Some felt forced into retirement while the rest had to interview for a position elsewhere because their jobs at our school had been forfeited by the school's closure. They lost contact with students, parents and colleagues with whom they'd build relationships. Just as the students and their parents had been, the faculty and staff became scattered dandelion seeds across the city.

These and other circumstances made me feel even more horribly about an impossible situation. I was damned if I complied with the directive and damned if I didn't because I'd become a pawn among "mean girls" in an injurious, high stakes chess match. I had no way to win the game at the time. This too is my truth. In order to walk in my truth, I must acknowledge what happened, speak my truth and ever dilute the magnitude of what happened to me or my school community so it won't happen to anyone else.

It doesn't matter what anyone thinks of or says about me because they haven't had to walk in my truth. They haven't cried themselves to sleep or agonized about my life. They don't know the full story of my breakthrough. It's the same for you.

You must choose defiance and stand for your truth, not only for your benefit but also to help others. People hate others for a portion of who they think that person is or what they did without knowing the sum total of who we are or what or circumstances are. When we stop to think about it, none of us can watch a snapshot of anyone else's life and form an informed opinion. Don't allow anyone to water down your truth. Be who *you're* designed to be and learn from your mistakes. Your growth and development aren't dependent on what anyone else thinks of you or your journey.

As encouraging as it is to know His purpose for me is unshakable and as empowered as I feel to walk in my truth, my experiences have also provided a third crucial reminder. I'm further reminded how important it is to put all of my faith in God over anyone else. I've become less concerned with what others say about me in order to prioritize my focus on what He says and what He wants me to do. At the end of the day, someone will always have something negative to say and there's nothing we can do about that.

During my encounters with loss, abuse of power, coercion and pain, I learned intimately who my genuine friends were and who they weren't. My genuine friends loved me through it with nothing but love and zero judgment. They never asked probing questions but they listened compassionately when I was ready to talk. They cried with me. They spoke up in my defense whether in my presence or behind my back . These friends represented true blessings. I also learned lessons. Some of my acquaintances, in an attempt to "get the tea," tried to cozy up to me. Many colleagues who thought I had positive relationships with gossiped about me as if I was the scourge of the earth based on what they'd heard through idle gossip and random tidbits about my personal business from the leaking sieve of the Internal Affairs Division. Some of them called me a whore, an idiot and stupid among so many other ugly insults. Part of me felt intensely pressured to clear my name while the rest of me wanted to hide and disappear.

Even some of my family members have had countless negative things to say, as if they were paying my bills when they never raised a hand to support me. You always believe your family will bear you up and defend you. Sadly, some family members will gossip like cowards and celebrate your downfall as quickly as they would a stranger's without talking directly to you. Some of them called me lazy, spoiled and entitled. They told other family members I wasn't looking for a job, that I didn't want to work. None of their idle gossip is true and it was hurtfully disappointing because they knew the real story and yet chose to treat me disdainfully and sit in judgment. Ironically, most of them failed to extend tangible help or support but they gave judgment so freely. Little did I know their judgment would become a gift. Experiences like these were so hurtful but they helped me at the same time by building strength and fortitude within me I never knew I had. I've learned to look adversity in the face and recognize it, even when it came from the most familiar faces that should have loved me and treated me differently. These family members blessed me while treating me spitefully and I'm grateful for it. I have become more emotionally intelligent and familiar with the landscape. Those who are closest to us often hurt us the most. As DMX said, "The snakes, the grass too long to see, The lawnmower sittin' right next to the tree." Now I know exactly who I'm dealing with and I can love, forgive and move forward without regret or anger in all of my relationships.

It won't be any different for you in similar circumstances. Lean on and believe in those who support you unconditionally. Believe in their love and compassion. By the same token, when people betray or mistreat you, and they will, hold onto your faith and remember this too shall pass. Forgive them and move forward without the burden of hatred and bitterness. Those who are disloyal to you are part of the plan for our lives. It happened *for you*, not to you. Judas betrayed Jesus, a perfect man and His betrayal became our opportunity to receive salvation. You won't always see it coming. Keep pushing forward, remembering that all things work for your good. Put your unadulterated faith in Him, not in them. Believe me, He knows the pain and the beauty in betrayal from personal experience just as we do. As I processed my experiences in real time, watching the wheat in my life being separated from the tares, my pain transformed from hurt to acceptance to gratitude.

Think of it this way. Gaining perspective about those by whom we're surrounded is always an invaluable experience and knowing who to believe in steadfastly is crucial. There's a fourth valuable lesson. The only way to live in peace is to confront each of our obstacles. We have not been given spirits of fear. Instead, we are empowered with love, power and the spiritual gift of self-control. Initially, this trio of police abuse and intimidation, coercion and abuse of power terrified me. Paralyzed by fear, I was afraid to speak out. Knowing people have been murdered by police for far less, I shrunk, withering like a raisin in the sun. I tried to hide but the more I tried to hide, the more unbearable it became. We have to pick our battles wisely. There are battles within battles and no matter how simple a situation seems to an onlooker, there's almost always an onion to peel when we're fighting our personal battles.

I've yearned to tell my story for years and it's taken a decade to become brave enough to finish writing it and to share what happened to me. One factor made me most fearful about sharing my testimony – the intense shame I felt. Shame and the ensuing humiliation it caused became a millstone around my neck. It weighed me down and prevented me from speaking out for far too long. My preoccupation with what people would think horrified me to my core. I wasn't sure I would survive the oppression of anyone's judgment and the deeper root of pain it would cause. Once I accepted that I had to confront my fears, my apprehension intensified because I'd kept a dark secret that haunted me. My fear of judgment and ridicule prevented me from sharing my testimony and helping others who've also been bitten by the reptile of police abuse and corruption. What would heal me and help others became an unavoidable step.

Years of sleepless nights, tear-stained pillowcases and a melancholy, self-imposed isolation established a deep layer of shame. I indulged my shame for wallowing in secrecy and languishing in the fear of what people would say. This brings me to a fifth important lesson. I had to stop basking in self-pity and choose to focus on the transformative power of my challenges so I could recover and uplift others. Self-pity made me a victim and caused me to turn inward, so bogged down with negative emotions that prevented me from moving forward. Once I pushed my self-pity aside, I could see I wasn't as defeated as I once believed I was. I became encouraged to fight back and seek my victory.

Trust me, I had every reason to feel angry, bitter and depressed. I'd been punished repeatedly for my personal choices and my personal life despite it being no one else's business. Even when I relocated six hours away for a new beginning, my experiences followed me like the stench from a skunk's behind. Entrapped in an excruciating situation created by overreaching leaders and their interloping informant who played with my life as carelessly as a kite skipping idly in the wind, I felt completely helpless. Wouldn't you be in agony if powerful people used your mistakes as a guillotine to end your career and subsequently dismember you once you tried to move on? Yet, I didn't have the right to remain angry, bitter and depressed. Those negative emotions held me back.

Yet, during these perpetual moments of turbulence molded and matured me exponentially. First, I experienced the depth and width of God's love for the first time. I'd never realized I needed Him more before this experience - and He was *there*. Of course He always loved me, had always been there, even when I made mistakes. Now I truly believed it. This difficult period of cyclonic upheaval that cut me so deeply began to bless me abundantly. I began realizing He had always been with me, especially when I planned to commit suicide. He sent angels of intervention who thwarted my plan to end my life. My lowest moments of pain and shame provided me with an Ephesians 3: 18-19 experience. In His wisdom and love, He used my shame to draw me closer to Him.

As He drew me closer *to* Him, I became stronger *in* Him because of the personal relationship I developed with Him during my worst times. I realized I'm nothing without Him and that it was His love I'd always needed and yet never pursued as relentlessly as I should have so many years before. Now, because He used my pain and shame for my good, I realize I'm purposed to share my story for His glory.

God's love strengthens me to tell my story *despite* being fearful at times. This is my opportunity to use my story to overcome every fear and break the chains to my past. It's also a platinum opportunity to encourage others who are grappling with life-changing circumstances. Throughout this journey of healing and even still occasionally, I've continuously reminded myself not to lose sight of my purpose. When I feel that lump of intimidation in my throat or palpitations in my heart, I reflect with assuredness that since God is *with me*, no one can defeat me. This belief, based on Romans 8:3, has propelled me through doubts and fears, strengthening me when I need it most.

You can face your fears too. The pain and hardships you've experienced have made you wiser and stronger. They've made you the person you've become. Your growth prepares you to love and support someone who needs you. Our nation and world are in the conditions they're in because too many of us are afraid to speak up for ourselves. We cannot continue to enlarge a culture of fear. We don't deserve it and our children don't either.

Choose defiance. Speak your truth. Don't allow anyone to make you choke on a meal prepared by their actions. As Maya Angelou once said, "Courage is the most important part of all the virtues, because without courage, you can't practice any other virtue consistently. You can practice any virtue erratically but nothing consistently without courage." Courage can help you overcome insecurity, timidity and doubt. If I'm courageous enough to share the obstacles I've overcome, you can too!

Once I stopped hating myself for my mistakes and no longer drowning in self-pity and guilt, I learned a sixth lesson. I realized I had to dwell on every positive in my life no matter how tiny it seemed to be. Some days I focused on how grateful I was to wake up. Other days my gratitude list increased. After nearly six months, I developed such a habit of looking for positives that it became an effortless reaction. This habit transformed my life and became an existential wakeup call. I realized my life hadn't ended, I'd simply encountered a major plot twist.

My dear friend Anthony asked me why I chose to name this book I Chose Defiance. I explained that the pain, shame and regret I felt nearly destroyed me, even planting a temporary desire to die until I became resolute to speak my truth. Life will never be all we want it to be nor will it provide all we need. Add to that the burdensome guilt and shame I felt before because I'd been so focused on what I wanted, I failed to recognize the myriad possibilities I could receive. It wasn't until I used all of the pain, humiliation and degradation for my good that I began to believe things would be alright. At present, I reflect on Jeremiah 29:11, reminding myself that God has plans for a bright future for me. I began to believe perhaps the negativity would be overcome by my faith and determination to seek Him.

It can be the very same for you. Whatever you're enduring, you can also look at the positives in your situation, even if you only see one glimmer. Focus on what you see and I believe you will find many reasons to be grateful. I Thessalonians 5:18 advises us to be grateful in all circumstances and in Proverbs 23:18, we are reminded we have a future where our hope won't be cut off.

Pat Smith, an amazing speaker and writer and also a beautiful spirit with style and grace, said, "Your passion comes from that place that's caused you the greatest pain." How very right Pat is. My pain has renewed and authenticated my purpose to be a servant leader. It's also created a fiery passion to inspire and motivate people to overcome their pain and use it to help others. We've all experienced pain. Pain is universal. How can you use your pain to move forward? What have you learned and what lessons are you continually learning that provide a new foundation to build on? It won't be easy or painless but I guarantee it's worth it.

The seventh and perhaps most difficult lesson is learning to cope with pain and agony we didn't bring on ourselves. My cousin Ricky had a horrific car accident that was not his fault. He's blessed to have survived the accident. The other driver's carelessness and substance abuse caused Ricky to undergo multiple surgeries and agonizing pain. My cousin Joi, his wife, and their daughters received this distressing news and it shattered them. What I admire about Ricky most is the rapidity with which he forgave the person who hit him so carelessly.

Ricky did in a week or two what it took me almost a year to do – forgive the one who hurt him. He never became embittered or enraged. Years ago, I wouldn't have been able to understand his response but after my own experience, I better understand the duality of forgiveness and love. We must forgive not only for the other person but also for ourselves. There is incredible power in forgiveness and loving others and it requires us to be brave and authentic. I wasn't initially brave enough to forgive the experiences I endured and it hurt me, not anyone who hurt me. While I felt angry and resentful, both natural and understandable responses, I held onto those negative emotions all too long while those who wronged and hurt me went on with their lives without a second thought about me or what they'd done to me. In essence, I stole my own joy through my inability to forgive and move on.

I'm the first to admit from experience that it isn't easy to release pain. When I reflect on the pain and regret I've lived through, I know what it's like to struggle, to vacillate between hopefulness and bleakness. I'm a living witness to the iron grip pride and stubbornness can have when we need to move forward. What we must do is realize that pride and an unforgiving attitude rather than the actual offense itself hold us back and prevent us from living happy, fulfilling lives.

After living in anger a little over a year, I complained, whined and remained stuck in a losing position. A pivotal conversation with my father changed my perspective. My father, a very forthright man who loved me with his entire heart, told me he was done listening to me gripe and grumble about my circumstances. It pained him how I dwelled in negativity and his heart ached because of it. He told me that I'd been a successful educator but that I couldn't remain stuck in the past, that I had skills and talents I could use differently. He advised me to speak life, exercise my faith and use my God-given talents to move forward. My eyes watered. My face burned. Hands shaking, I ended our conversation.

Daddy stunned me when he spoke to me so harshly. He'd always comforted me when I was in pain, encouraging me to believe everything would work out in the end. Initially, I thought he was ignoring how unkindly and unfairly I'd been treated. Reflecting on our conversation throughout the day, I realized Daddy was right. He didn't negate my feelings. He wanted me to realize things wouldn't ever change if my attitude didn't improve. He wanted me to leave my self-imposed prison of unforgiveness, self-pity and shattered hopes. Ultimately, Daddy wanted me to get out of my own way. Our pivotal conversation led to my most life-changing epiphany, that *for my own happiness* and future, I had to forgive, show my faith and renew my hopes. I remember Matthew 5:44, where we're advised to love our enemies and pray for those who hurt us.

    I began to choose life and light again. Each day it's up to me to choose happiness, light and love. Nothing changed for me overnight. I became ore faithful and persevering while I faced foreclosure, bouts of depression about long-term unemployment, heart disease, getting fit and healthier without healthcare, suicidal tendencies along with life's routine challenges. During the time I remained hidden, God prepared me for my ultimate purpose, to encourage each of you with my story.

    My story and experiences make me broken but beautifully made whole like so many other extraordinary people I know and love. When I reflect on my experiences and how God has loved me through it all and rebuilt me from ashes, I often think of the Japanese tradition of repairing broken objects by filling the cracks and broken edges with gold. By doing this, the Japanese take great care to ensure the flaw is uniquely preserved and it also adds to the object's beauty. What a remarkable tradition! Imagine how beautifully whole each of us become when we treasure our brokenness and the lessons that come from it rather than hiding in secrecy, shame and fear. Remarkable things happen when we confess our flaws and share our experiences to guide others along their paths to healing and wholeness. Use your pain and lessons to heal yourself and then help others. You won't regret it and you'll be unimaginably blessed as a result. Allow love, light and learning to be the gold that fills your cracks.

ACKNOWLEDGEMENTS

There are many people who've supported me through the past decade and during the time I spent writing and editing this book. Much devotion to my mother for her love, support, and encouragement. She never doubted me. Love and light in memory of my father for his reassurance and dedication that everything would be alright. He reminded me that while justice takes time, it always comes around. I surely do miss you, Daddy.

Many thanks to the incredible renaissance man who pushes, encourages and supports me, who refuses to allow me to give up on myself when I'm afraid or feeling doubts. Above everything else we share, our friendship and teamwork mean most.

Love and appreciation to my Soror and friend Donna M. N. Edwards, J.D., for her editing skills and for writing the foreword. Deep gratitude to my mentor Doris Reed for providing guidance and wise counsel since 2002. Appreciation to Prince George's County Delegate Michael A. Jackson for giving me an educational consulting job when no one else would and for his mentorship over the past decade.

A extra special thank you from a grateful heart to my sisters Renita Chapell, Lynette Yancey, Natalie Kay, Lisa Muhammad, Natasha Reid, Angela Holmes, Lisa Smith-Sherrod, Kirsten White, Anesa Johnson, Katrina Stokes Dudley, LaShan Haynes, DeVon Hall and Nekeyyah Blount

Jackson. Love and gratitude also to my Sorors Yottie Kenan Smalls, Judith Fitzgerald, Crystal Wilson Davis, Julie Jones, Diana Durham Bowden, Wendy Morancie, Tarama Giles, Denise Jackson, Tracey Strong, Nicole Edwards and Shaunia Wallace Carlyle. Each of these ladies cheered me on, listened when I cried or wanted to scream, they've supported all of my writing projects and uplifted me through every loss I've grown through over the past decade. I love and appreciate each of you! There are other phenomenal women who've supported me too and I'm eternally grateful for each of them. If I could name each of you, I would. As my father often told people, I appreciate each of you to the highest!!

 I'm grateful to Anwar Golladay and my Myoflexfit gym family for helping me to get my mind and body in better condition. It isn't easy to stick to a physical fitness plan but a dedicated gym family makes it much easier. Special thanks also to my big little brother Remington Seales who pushes me to lift heavier and steadier and who tells you the blunt truths you need to hear. The journey isn't over and I'm excited and grateful to see it through.

 Thank you to Robert Dennis, my business consultant and principal of The Krimson Group, LLC, for encouraging me to expand my original business plan to serve even more people. I'm also grateful for his prayers and moral support.

I must thank Rudy Jules, a true brother to me. There are times he became a guardian angel of sorts and saved me from disaster. You don't meet many people as genuine as Rudy and for him, I'm grateful.

Special thanks to the talented people who made my book cover and concept come to life. Jaida A. Moore of Jaida A. Photography took a photo example and brought the look I wanted to life. Natasha Reid of Reid Artistry provided makeup artistry that I'm still admiring. Devon Hall styled my hair to perfection. Tracey Strong provided styling services that completed my look perfectly. Dennis Beckwith designed the cover with ideal graphics.

To anyone I've forgotten to thank, please charge it to my head and not my heart.

Love,
Carol

Made in the USA
Middletown, DE
23 August 2018